The Thyme Bandit
Cook Book

The
Thyme Bandit
Cook Book

Recipes from White Star Farms and a lifetime of cooking

from Alaska to Antarctica and all places in between.

By Sharon Samuels

Copyright © 2014 Sharon Samuels

Illustrations © 2014 Sharon Samuels

All rights reserved

Published in the United States by

Tucker Trading

ISBN: 978-0-69221-538-8

Printed by CreateSpace

Design by Sharon Samuels

First Edition

For my mom who said, "Cooking is your art".

TABLE OF CONTENTS

Preface

XI

Introduction

XIII

Pantry Notes

1

Appetizers

7

Breakfast

27

Salad Dressings

51

Salads

61

Soups and Sandwiches

79

Sides

101

Pasta & Pizza

119

Entrées

145

Desserts

171

Recipe & DF, GF, V Index

191

Heirloom Index

197

Preface

Over the years, people I have worked with and for, and cooked with and for have encouraged me to write a cookbook. While living on the farm, I finally took the suggestions seriously and began an outline. However, my work on the farm did not leave many hours in a day to write on a cookbook project. The basic outline I had created sat in a folder on a yellow memo notepad with an occasional addition here and there over the next few years.

In the summer of 2013, having left the farm behind to return to Alaska, I began the project again, typing away in my cabin at a remote Alaskan lodge Jeff and I were managing. But as it turns out, like farming, lodge management left little spare time for my project. For the most part that summer, I was only able to transfer my outline from the yellow memo notepad into a word document on the computer.

Skip forward to the winter of 2013/14 when our winter work plans to return to Antarctica fell through at the last minute. Back home in Girdwood, Alaska, after traveling in the fall and with no job, I jumped back into the cookbook project. As the winter wore on, I began to work in town but took ten minutes here and an hour there to slowly keep the project moving forward. And this time it did and so here I am, finally with a cookbook to share with you all.

Cook on,

Sharon Samuels

Late Summer 2014

Introduction

There is a little cardboard print which hangs in my kitchen and says, "never enough thyme". The saying is surrounded by a cartoon drawing of two quilted angels. One angel is holding a clay pot of thyme and the other has a bird nesting in her hair. A large flowering vine outlines the angels and looks as though it is growing from their feet. Small cartoon birds collect nectar from the flowers on the vine and butterflies fill the rest of the empty space. "Never enough thyme", this must be the oldest joke in the kitchen. At every cooking job I have ever had and in every kitchen of my own, there has lived a "Thyme Bandit" who has persistently appropriated my time.

My life has been filled with kitchens, rarely one that has been big or fancy. In my dorm room I used a coffee maker to make noodles, truly one of the least effective ways of doing so. My first cabin in Alaska had no running water but it did have a dorm fridge which was often warmer on the inside than the whole cabin when I came home from work. On the boat there was a perfect horseshoe galley with a picture window above the sink. That sink, however, had a limited amount of water available to use during the time spent away from the docks. The standard Japanese kitchen which I used in our home in Asahikawa for three years, had just a sink, a two burner gas stove with a fish broiler underneath and a 2' x2' work space in between. In Antarctica, again I had no running water and also no refrigerator. Out on the ice sheet there is an art to keeping things cold but not frozen. Instead of a counter, the Antarctic kitchen had a large folding office table for a work space and, whenever I needed it, a whisk you could attach to a power drill. Our first house felt like it was built by a bachelor and some dudes. When finished, they realized there was no refrigerator in which to put their beer. So they bought an old mustard yellow number and pushed it into the linen closet, ran an extension cord through a hole drilled in the floor, across the entire basement and plugged it in to an available outlet above what happened to be the most magnificent work bench my husband has ever had. Then, since a fridge needs a kitchen, they added a small counter, a sink, a second small counter and, in front of the 4'x4' picture window which looked over a muskeg meadow and out onto a magnificent uninhabited Alaskan ridge, they put a tiny stove. The farm had a small horseshoe kitchen about the same size as onboard the boat and just a little smaller than my current condo kitchen here in Alaska.

In each one of these kitchens, and in many others, I have disregarded any number of additional life activities in order to spend my time cooking. At the end of each week I have turned over many hours with food to the Thyme Bandit. I have thought about food, written about it, watched cooking programs, read countless books and magazines about food, planned cooking adventures, cleaned up after kitchen successes and failures, shopped, tasted, smelled, and touched food.

What I have learned over the years is that what in fact makes cooking work so well is not at all the kitchen. Instead it is twofold in both the time you spend cooking and the ingredients you have to use. When I say "time spent cooking", I mean cooking as a total package. Not just in a kitchen but also the shopping, tasting, smelling, reading, planning and thinking about food which happens before you get into the kitchen. When I say "ingredients", I mean the very best and the most basic foods you can get your hands on.

I know not everyone has either the time or the desire to spend on cooking as a total package. You can however take advantage of my offerings to the Thyme Bandit by enjoying the recipes in this book. It is a collection of my memories and experiences from kitchens and travels and food related jobs around the world translated into recipes for you to enjoy. In the end however, no matter where you are cooking and what ingredients you have to use there is "never enough thyme" to complete all the possible kitchen adventures. And that will always keep cooking exciting for me.

Pantry Notes

You can find numerous articles recommending what to keep on hand in your pantry. I have several torn out of magazines and tucked into my folder of recipes. In the early days of having my own kitchen, and having the ability to stock it how I chose, I would look over these articles and then go to the store to pick up various items. Doing so would slowly build up my pantry which would come close to, but never quite meet the robust suggestions noted in the articles.

As the years have gone by I have settled into a few major staples with odds and ends showing up periodically as I tackle various cooking adventures. My pantry at home may be lacking in some respects when compared to these articles however, more importantly, it reflects how I cook. And yours should too. The commercial pantries I have cooked from while working various jobs much better reflect the suggested stores from these articles and are terrifically fun to cook from. At home, space, cost and what I really actually cook on a regular basis take precedence. Below is, for the most part, how I keep my pantry.

Herbs

Fresh – Selected from your own garden, window box, deck pots or the farmers market whenever possible. Otherwise, I buy a clamshell of organic herbs at the store. Selecting one of the 'blend' options gives a variety of herbs without waste. My favorites to have on hand are **thyme, sage, rosemary, cilantro** and **Italian parsley.**

Dried – These are best purchased in small useable quantities from the bulk department. By "useable", I mean the amount you will use up in a couple of months or the amount you need for an unusual recipe you are making. This keeps the dried herbs in your cupboard fresh. For the most part, I only keep dried **basil** and **oregano**. They are great for red sauces, salad dressings, soups and beans.

Spices

As with the herbs, the dried spices are best when purchased in small useable quantities from the bulk department bins. I keep **ground cumin, ground turmeric, smoked paprika, sweet paprika, granulated garlic, ground cinnamon, cardamom seeds,** coriander seeds, bay leaves, one whole nutmeg, whole coriander, crushed red peppers, black peppercorns, finely ground black pepper** and **ground white pepper.**

Salt

Kosher – I use **kosher salt** when cooking on the stove top (sauté, egg cookery, soups, sauces), for sprinkling on top of baked goods or salads, for meat (on the stovetop, in the oven, on the grill) and for all kinds of finishing (a sprinkle of salt before serving).

Table – I use **table salt** in recipes when baking.

Flavored/Other – I always keep **celery salt** on hand for making soups, salad dressings and cooking poultry. Celery salt also makes a great appetizer for Belgian style beers if you sprinkle some over chunks of plain Gouda cheese. **Smoked salts** are a great addition to many dishes produced in the home kitchen and not outside on a grill. My favorite is alder smoked salt. **Fleur de sel** or **Maldon** are both very nice finishing sea salts. It is my preference is to have at least one of these on hand at all times.

Oil

EVOO – Currently, I purchase a Californian **extra virgin olive oil** because it is as local as we can get here in Alaska and I like the flavor. I use it for dressings when the flavor of olive oil is preferential and for finishing soups, making pizzas, drizzling on popcorn and finishing sauces.

Olive Oil – A light **olive oil** with a light flavor I use for all other oil needs.

Other Oil – The only other oil I use with any regularity is **dark roasted sesame oil.** The flavor is unmistakable and exquisite when used in the right place in the right time.

Vinegar

White and Red – One bottle of plain **white vinegar** and one nice bottle of **red wine vinegar** for baking, salads, sauces, dressings, pickling and cleaning.

Balsamic – Always have one basic good quality **balsamic** for salads, sauces and dressings. When it is an option to get a treat for the pantry, I do like to have one **ancient balsamic** for salads, finishing and desserts.

Apple Cider – An **apple cider** vinegar with a 'mother' is great for salad dressings, salsas, stir-fry, chutneys/relishes, and general health.

Rice Wine – **Seasoned rice wine** vinegar is maybe my greatest weakness for processed food in my kitchen. It is rice vinegar which has been salted and sugared. The ease of making a salad dressing with this single ingredient borders on ridiculous.

Canned

Vegetables - When I was canning on the farm, all I bothered with were **tomatoes** and **pickles**. And the tomatoes were only ever whole peeled tomatoes. When I do not have those on hand, I keep 28 oz cans of whole peeled tomatoes in the cupboard. Other than that, just some roasted chilies.

Fruit - **Peaches** or **apricots** from a can are great for a quick last minute dessert if you have no fresh fruit around.

Fish – Canned albacore (white) or skipjack **tuna** (U.S. troll or pole caught) and canned Alaskan wild caught **salmon** are not only great for cold sandwich salads but also for turning into fish cakes at the last minute.

Frozen

Vegetables - Naturally on the farm, whatever would not keep on its own in cold storage was tossed into the freezer. I would blanch the leafy greens, roast tomatoes/peppers/eggplant, cook and puree pumpkin, and shred the summer squash. Off the farm I usually keep only frozen **peas** and **corn**.

Fruit – Whatever **berries** I can get my hands on go into the freezer. **Rhubarb** is also great to have in the freezer. Along with any over abundant fresh **peaches** that have been blanched, peeled and sliced.

Fresh Food

What I mean by "fresh food" is food you can get from "still growing" to "in your mouth" in the shortest amount of time. Food harvested at the peak of ripeness and eaten as soon as possible, in my experience, is always better than food that has traveled. The more food you can get fresh from your own garden, a family garden, a community garden or your friend's garden, the better. The next best option is your local farmers market or a local CSA box of food delivered to your neighborhood for pick-up.

Dried

Beans/Legumes - Typically, I only keep **black beans, garbanzo beans, cannellini beans** and **lentils** in the pantry. Other beans or legumes I pick up at the store when I am making a special recipe.

Pasta - I select pasta at the store based upon the recipe I intend to make. Or I will succumb to marketing when a fancy pasta shape in a pretty package catches my eye. **Orecchiette, Israeli couscous, tortellini, soba** and **angel hair** are some of my favorites.

Rice - To keep up with cooking food from around the world I like to have **sushi rice, brown rice, basmati rice** and **jasmine rice** in the pantry.

Grains – **Steel cut oats, old fashioned oatmeal, polenta** and **popcorn** round out the grains I keep stocked in the cupboard.

Meat/Fish/Seafood

When buying meat, fish or seafood, buy the best you can afford, as fresh as you can find it from the most reputable source.

Dairy/Cheese

Read the label. The lowest number of ingredients your sour cream, cottage cheese, cream cheese etc., contain the better. Remember, big yellow blocks of cheese are not the only highly processed dairy products on the market! When selecting milk for recipes I choose the least processed option available to me at the time of need.

I like to keep a couple of **cheeses for slicing** for a cheese platter, a brick of **cream cheese** for last minute appetizers/desserts/recipes and one big hunk of **parmesan reggiano** in the cheese drawer. Otherwise I select my cheese purchases based upon what recipe I am making and then try to purchase only the quantity I need.

Other

This is a list of other items I use frequently and always keep in the kitchen: **baking powder, baking soda, cornstarch, white flour, wheat flour, buckwheat flour, almond flour, cornmeal, cocoa powder, panko, nori, honey, maple syrup, white sugar, brown sugar, buttermilk powder, soy sauce, nutritional yeast powder,**

vermouth, lemon juice, ketchup, mayonnaise, hot sauce, mustard, vanilla, dry active yeast, peanut butter, jam, miso, butter, shortening, coconut milk, rice/soy milk, and sourdough starter.

Heirlooms

Throughout the cookbook, I note my favorite heirloom produce variety in recipes. Some of these you will be able to find in a regular grocery store, others in a fancy grocery store and some only at your local farmers market or in your own garden. Heirloom produce are varieties which by common definition, existed prior to WWII and due to their excellent flavor, have been repeatedly seed saved by generations of home gardeners and small farmers. These varieties do not always travel well. They may be susceptible to wilting quickly after harvest or have soft and easily damaged skin. They also may have a low fruit to plant ratio or be difficult to pick which inhibits production, processing and return on investment for larger growers. Heirlooms are however delicious and worth the effort to grow or the money spent to purchase.

At anytime you can substitute a non-heirloom variety.

Naughty Food

Just so you know, every once in a while I am fed up with the thyme bandit collecting hours of mine in the kitchen. And so yes, my pantry is also stocked with some quick-to-make-and-eat highly processed foods from the center aisles of the grocery store. Maybe we could call them comfort food. I like to eat them, sometimes just like I like to wear soft clothes at home sometimes. They most often are: 0.49 cent packages of ramen noodles (oriental flavor), corn tortilla chips, cream of mushroom soup in a can, macaroni and cheese, dark chocolate bars, yellow boxes of crackers, soft granola bars and little packages of fruit flavored chews.

APPETIZERS

Sumo Snacks

Pico de Gallo and Salsa

Mizuna Pesto with Ricotta on Crostini

Pita Wedges Two Ways

Roasted Red Pepper Spread

Rosemary Crackers with Goat Cheese and Fresh Plums

Grilled Eggplant Dip

Spring Radish Spread for Crackers and Crudités

Mushroom Gyoza

Pesto Cheese Bundles

Popcorn

Sumo Snacks

20 bite size snacks

When we were living in Japan, my husband Jeff became a fan of sumo wrestling. Every other month, for two weeks at a time there was a sumo tournament on television. Lower ranked wrestlers have their bouts earlier in the day while the top ranked wrestlers face off in the evening, just about the time Jeff returned home from work. In Japan, it is not uncommon to go to an Izakaya (Japanese pub) and order a few small plates of snacks to nibble on while enjoying a beer. This sumo snack is one I would often make for Jeff to have at home along with his beer during tournament time.

1 pkg egg roll wrappers

5 oz mozzarella cheese

¼ c olive oil

ketchup

Open the package of egg roll wrappers and cut into quarters. Re-wrap two quarters tightly in a bag and set aside for another time. Cut the cheese into ¼" x 1 ½" mini-logs. Separate a single ¼ sheet of egg roll wrapper and place it on the counter in front of you. Lay a cheese log across one corner. Dampen the inside edges of the wrapper with water to create a seal when you roll it up. Roll up the cheese log in the egg roll wrapper folding in the edges as you go. When you are finished it should look like a mini burrito. Repeat until all of the cheese logs have been rolled up in egg roll wrappers. In a deep fry pan, heat up the oil. When it is shimmering add several cheese burritos turning each one as to brown all four sides. When uniformly brown and the cheese is melted inside, remove from the pan and place on a paper towel lined plate to drain. Serve warm with ketchup for dipping.

Pico de Gallo and Salsa

Makes approximately 2 cups

With the wide array of salsa selections available in the supermarket, it may seem simpler to buy a product rather than make one at home. However, salsa prepared in your home kitchen is not only easy to do but also simple and delicious. I have included a preparation using only a knife and a few simple ingredients as well as a food processor method which produces a more complex, full-bodied salsa. At home we prefer the hand cut salsa when serving tacos, and food processor method when serving chips and dip or quesadillas.

Pico de Gallo

1 c diced seeded beefsteak tomato (such as Brandywine, Cherokee Purple or Moskvich)

¾ c diced white onion

½ jalapeño pepper diced fine

¼ c loosely packed chopped fresh cilantro

½ small lime

2 tbsp olive oil

¼ tsp salt

Mix the tomato, onion and cilantro together in a bowl. Juice the lime over the mixture and add the olive oil and salt. Mix again and let rest 5 minutes before serving. Check flavor and adjust seasoning before serving.

Salsa

1 quart jar of canned whole tomatoes (substitute one 28 oz. can whole tomatoes)

½ green pepper

½ white onion

1 jalapeño pepper

1 tsp salt

2 tsp cumin

1 tsp cider vinegar

2 cloves garlic

1 bunch cilantro

Drain the tomatoes and add them to the bowl of a food processor fitted with a chopping blade. Reserve the juice for another use. Halve the green pepper and remove the seeds and ribs from one side and add it to the food processor. Set aside the other half for another use. Halve the onion, peel off the outside and cut into large chunks and add them to the bowl of the food processor. Set aside the other half for another use. Remove the stem, seeds and ribs from the jalapeño and add it to the bowl of the food processor. Add the salt, cumin and vinegar to the food processor. Pulse the blade until uniformly chunky. Adjust seasonings to your taste. Wash the cilantro and remove the majority of the lower stems by slicing them off with a knife in one fell swoop. Add the cilantro to the bowl of the food processor and pulse until just incorporated. Serve with corn chips or quesadillas.

Mizuna Pesto with Ricotta on Crostini

40 crostini

Mizuna is a fantastic-to-look-at peppery mustard family green that is native to Japan. It is a wonderful salad green (see Mizuna and Tofu Salad pg. 68), an excellent addition to soup or stir fry and can be made into this wonderful pesto with so many uses. Look for Mizuna at your local farmers market or Asian food store that carries fresh vegetables.

1 lb Mizuna

½ c olive oil

¾ c walnuts

1 tbsp lemon juice

salt to taste

40 crostini

1 2/3 c ricotta cheese

Chop the mizuna into 4" pieces. Add all of the ingredients to the bowl of your food processor and pulse until finely chopped. On each slice of crostini, spread about 2 tsp of fresh ricotta. On top of the ricotta, spread about 1 tsp of mizuna pesto. Serve on a nice tray. Any leftover mizuna pesto you can freeze in an ice cube tray. Once the mizuna pesto has frozen, you can pop the cubes out into a plastic bag.

Other serving suggestions:

Mix with soft tofu for an alternative sandwich spread

Toss with your favorite pasta and some fresh diced tomatoes.

Add to your scrambled eggs.

Spread on a pizza.

Mix with rice wine vinegar to make a salad dressing.

Add to a creamy tomato soup.

Pita Wedges Two Ways

32 bite size snacks

During the time when Jeff and I were running our own heirloom vegetable farm, we would attend two markets a week to sell all of our produce. At each of these markets, not only were there a number of other farm-to-market stands but also a number of small direct market stands of any number of products from dog treats to jams and jellies to the hummus and pita guy. Now at the end of a long harvest and market day it was honestly hard to come home and cook anything at all to eat for dinner. And sometimes, we did stop at the burrito shop on the way home, but sometimes, we took home a pile of fresh made pitas and warmed it in the oven with a few simple toppings for a delicious addition to our farm salad dinner. These are also exceptional appetizers for a small dinner party.

1 package thick pitas (not pocket pitas)

1 small (7") Costata Romanesca (or any) zucchini sliced into THIN circles

2 thick slices of fresh mozzarella

8 large leaves of Genovese basil sliced into thin strips

2 Costata Romanesca zucchini blossoms (plucked fresh and barely open from a garden)

½ c shredded manchego (style of Spanish cheese, substitute any hard cheese)

2 tbsp finely chopped herbs (a mix of any of the following: chives, chive blossoms, thyme, marjoram, oregano, sage)

4 tbsp EVOO

1 tsp Fleur de sel salt (or a finishing salt of your choice)

Place 4 pitas flat side up on a baking sheet. Brush each with a generous layer of EVOO. On two of the pitas, lay a thick slice of fresh mozzarella in the very center. Then, starting at the outside of the pita, lay down overlapping rings of zucchini slices until you reach the mozzarella in the center. Using your fingers gently shred one zucchini blossom into strips over each of these pitas. Sprinkle the strips of basil over these pitas. On the two remaining pitas, sprinkle the Manchego cheese and the finely chopped herbs. Drizzle all four of the pitas with the remaining EVOO and sprinkle them with the kosher salt. Broil until sizzling and starting to brown. DON'T leave the broiling pitas unattended! Remove from oven, cool and slice with a pizza cutter into wedges. Serve as an appetizer or as a side to a nice big salad.

Roasted Red Pepper Spread for Crackers and Crudités

Makes approximately 1 ½ cups

Roasted food is extraordinarily delicious. For whatever reason, I can't recall the first time I ate a roasted red pepper. My best guess is that it was on top of some vegetarian style pizza, in college. More recently in Spain, I was treated to one roasted red pepper after another. This was most certainly because we happened to be in Spain during pepper roasting season. Roasted peppers were draped across any number of tiny appetizers. Roasted and gently sautéed peppers showed up day after day as a side dish. Oh and the paella with peppers, oh my how very, very good. One day, we walked into a town and there was an outdoor market. Keen on the food aspects of travel the idea of strolling through a market hit the spot. Well, this was no regular market. It was an entire market of booth after booth of only bright red peppers. Some hot, some sweet- all piled high on tables, in back of trucks and in baskets and bins on the ground. And then there was the smell of roasting peppers and roar of the burners of a half dozen roasting machines operating behind a booth here and a farm truck over there. Woe is me that I did not take a single picture. This recipe here is so quick and easy yet remains a crowd pleaser every single time I put it out on the table.

8 oz cream cheese

4 oz sour cream

1 roasted sweet red pepper (from a can or jar, or roasted on your stove top over an open flame or grilled slowly on your barbecue – skin, seeds, stem and veins removed see page 155 for guidelines)

Cream the cream cheese and sour cream together until uniform. Finely chop the red pepper and add to the cheese mixture along with any juices. Mix well. Serve with crackers and crudités.

Rosemary Crackers with Goat Cheese and Fresh Plums

40 bite size snacks

If you can wander through your local farmers market and come away with fresh goat cheese, some locally made rosemary crackers and bright, juicy sun-ripened plums, you have hit the jackpot! A number of years ago, before starting our own farm, Jeff and I spent a month working with a good friend of ours on her farm in Bozeman. The little Wednesday market culture was as good as you could imagine with music, food carts, farmers and other vendors serving to the locals who would walk and bike from the neighborhoods with their families and friends in tow. The park and pavilion would slowly fill to capacity with weekly shoppers filling their baskets and then pausing on the lawn to eat dinner, listen to music and watch the kids play on the playground. What better way to spend a summer afternoon and evening. It was here that I was first blissed out by eating homemade rosemary crackers with fresh goat cheese. Later, when working the markets outside of Portland, Oregon, I made the addition of fresh plums to this treat and simply could not be happier while eating this ultimate food combination.

40 rosemary crackers (from the market, homemade or from the store)

8 oz goat cheese

10 fresh purple Italian prunes(or other fresh plum) cut into quarters

Spread each cracker with 2 tsp goat cheese. Add one slice of plum. Serve.

Grilled Eggplant Dip

Makes approximately 2 cups

Love or hate the taste: fresh, whole eggplant is always a beautiful sight. More often than any other vegetable here in America, eggplant is prepared poorly and the results are not satisfying. This recipe is simple and it is worth the time to prepare. When working outside during the day on the farm, I would start a charcoal fire in our outdoor dome grill. Once the coals were hot and ready, I would load the grill with fresh picked eggplant, put the lid on and leave the whole thing alone for the rest of the day, except for one visit to rotate all the eggplant. Before heading inside for the evening, I would collect the eggplant from the grill. The outsides would be charred and wrinkled with splits in the skin where rivulets of caramelized juices bubbled out. The flesh inside had transformed from white and spongy to caramel colored, smoky flavored, silky smooth and easy to scoop out with a spoon. Some I would prepare to eat right away and the rest I would freeze to use later in the winter. If you try this recipe and like it, grill more eggplant than you need next time so you can freeze it for a later use.

> 4 Rosa Bianca eggplants (each about the size of a baseball or an equivalent amount)*
>
> 1 tsp lemon juice
>
> 2 cloves garlic
>
> 1 tsp kosher salt
>
> 1 package thick pitas (about 5, toast and cut into wedges)

Grill** eggplant whole until soft and mushy all over inside (up to 1 hour depending upon the heat of your grill and the size of your eggplant). Cool completely. Remove outer charred skin and put eggplant pulp into a Cuisinart. For every one cup of eggplant pulp add ½ tsp salt, ½ tsp lemon juice and 1 clove garlic. Pulse until pureed. Check for seasoning and adjust to taste. Serve with toasted wedges of pita bread or corn chips.

* Farmers markets or Asian grocery stores should have reasonable sizes of eggplant. The very large purple variety sold in many grocery stores is a little too big and should be cut down into 3rds or quarters. Any exterior skin which gets charred while being cooked will be discarded.

** Alternatives to grilling are roasting in your oven or charring over a gas burner on top of your stove. Both work well but take more of your time and do not leave the eggplant infused with that wonderful smokey flavor. You can always add a drop or two of liquid smoke to the final recipe. Roasting in the oven works best if you have long narrow Asian style eggplant. Coat them lightly with oil and set on a half sheet pan in an oven turned up to at least 450 degrees. Roll the eggplant over after about 30 minutes. Leave them in the oven until soft and squishy from top to tail. If you are going to char the eggplant over a gas burner on your stove be sure to turn on the fan first and have a pair of metal tongs. This also works much better on long and narrow eggplant. Turn on the burner or grill insert and place the clean and dry eggplant over the flames by balancing them on top of a burner or grill insert. Keep the flame low enough that it slowly browns and chars the skin rather than setting it on fire. Rotate the eggplant so all surface areas are equally exposed to the heat. Continue to do so until the eggplant is soft and mushy and the entire outer surface is charred. Allow to cool and continue with the recipe.

Spring Radish Spread

Makes approximately 1 ½ cups

I say "Spring radish spread" because one of the very first vegetables to pop up in the Spring and be ready to eat is the radish. Never one keen on a radish in a salad, I found on the farm I was always on the look-out for a new way to use these pretty little veggies and keep them from crowding out everything else in the fridge. Here is a lovely spread for crackers, crudités, or for a summer sandwich with cucumbers and salad greens.

4 oz cream cheese

3 tbsp plain yogurt

1 clove garlic

2 Evergreen Hardy White scallions or a bunch of chives

2/3 c French breakfast radish (chopped)

½ tsp smoked paprika

½ tsp kosher salt

¼ tsp fresh cracked pepper

In a medium sized bowl cream the cream cheese and yogurt together until smooth. Crush the garlic and finely chop the green onions or chives and mix into the cream cheese mixture. Finely chop the radish and mix well into spread. Add salt, pepper and smoked paprika. Taste and adjust for seasoning. Serve with crackers and crudités or spread onto a sandwich.

Mushroom Gyoza

40 bite size snacks

"Gyoza" in Japanese, or frozen-out-of-a-bag pot stickers; no matter what you call them, they are delicious. While they do take time to make, you can easily prepare them ahead and freeze them for use later. These are often served as a side dish although I do have one memorable experience where we joined some friends at their home and proceeded to make nothing but gyoza for our dinner. We each probably ate two dozen over the course of the evening. Cook, eat, cook some more, eat, then drink some sake or beer and cook some more gyoza to eat. Below is the basic mushroom gyoza we made that night adjusted for ingredients you can find easily here in the U.S.A.

12 large fresh shitake (or crimini) mushrooms

1 bunch nira (or Evergreen Hardy White scallions or green onions)

1 medium Danvers carrot

2" fresh ginger

3 cloves garlic

1 ½ c Napa cabbage (or green cabbage)

1 tbsp olive oil

1 tbsp kosher salt

1 tbsp sesame oil

2 tsp corn starch

1 package gyoza wrappers (round)

To make the stuffing in the bowl of a Cuisinart fitted with the sharp cutting blade, place the shitake, nira, peeled carrot broken into 3 pieces, peeled ginger sliced into about 4 rings, peeled garlic, roughly chopped napa cabbage and the kosher salt. Pulse the vegetables until they are finely chopped. You may have to remove the lid of the Cuisinart several times and push the larger chunks down towards the blades. Heat the olive oil in a 12" skillet and add the vegetables from the Cuisinart. Sauté until the mushrooms are soft and fragrant. Open the package of gyoza wrappers and have a small bowl of water on hand. Before filling each wrapper, run your damp finger along the outer edge of one half of the wrapper (drawing a damp "C" on the outer edge). Place about 2 tsp of stuffing into each wrapper. Fold the wrapper in half over the filling and starting at one edge pinch closed the edges. The damp edge will adhere to the dry edge. As you are pinching introduce 'ruffles" in the wrapper and pinch them into the edges (about 5 'ruffles' per gyoza) this will give them the "look" you will recognize when you are finished. Set them firmly on a cookie sheet giving them a flat bottom.

Once all of the gyozas have been formed, you can choose to freeze, boil or fry them. To freeze, simply place the cookie sheet into your freezer overnight. The next morning, knock each gyoza loose and store in an airtight freezer container. To boil, bring a large pot of water to a rolling boil. Add the gyoza (the number depends upon the size of your pot, they should be able to move around freely in the boiling water) and when they bounce up to the top and float, they are finished. If you boil the frozen gyoza it will take a few minutes longer than the fresh made gyoza. Scoop out the floating gyoza and set them on a rack to "drip dry" before putting them on a serving plate. To fry the gyoza, heat 1 tbsp of toasted sesame oil over medium heat in a large skillet. Add the gyoza flat side down and fry until the bottom is crisp. While the gyozas are frying in the skillet, mix ¼ cup of water with 2 tablespoons of cornstarch. Stir until milky and add about 3 tablespoons of this mixture to the pan around the gyoza, lower the heat and cover with a lid for a few minutes. This will allow the rest of the gyoza to steam cook. The gyoza should be all stuck together when you loosen them from the skillet. Serve warm with a dipping sauce made from sweetened rice wine vinegar and a few drops of either toasted sesame oil or chili oil.

Pesto Cheese Bundles

25 bite-sized snacks

We used to make these in the tiny kitchen at the back of the lodge during my first cooking job in Alaska. The kitchen looked just like what you would find in any cabin here in Alaska. A mustard colored stove, a sink, cupboards made out of boards held together by black iron fixtures, a low ceiling, a big piece of mosquito netting stapled over the window and a slanted floor. To make cooking for all the guests at the lodge easier, a second kitchen was added next to the first. It was a little more modern looking in that it had white appliances and a commercial dish sanitizer. Both of the ovens we had on hand were gas fired and most certainly required turning the pans during cooking. In fact, some of the recipes we used even said as much ("half way through baking turn the cookies"). One day I remember a helper in the kitchen pulling the pan of cookies out of the oven and flipping each cookie upside down like a pancake before putting them back in the oven! If you have a good oven yourself, no need to turn the pesto cheese bundles, just keep an eye on them so they do not all burst open. If they do, don't worry, while they may not be as pretty on an appetizer platter, they will be just as delicious.

1 sheet puff pastry thawed according to package directions

2 tbsp pesto (homemade or from a jar)

½ c shredded mozzarella cheese

1 egg

In a small mixing bowl stir the pesto and mozzarella cheese. In another small bowl, whisk the egg. Lay out the sheet of puff pastry and gently roll into a 10"x10" square. Using a 2" round biscuit cutter cut out 25 rounds from the puff pastry. Place one tsp of pesto/cheese mixture onto each round. Fold each round in half and pinch together the very edges tucking in any errant piece of cheese. Place these bundles onto a cookie sheet. Using a small tined fork, press around each pinched-together edge, giving each pastry a decorative look. With a pastry brush wash each pastry with egg. Bake in a 400 degree oven for approximately 5 minutes. Serve warm.

Popcorn

1 bowl full

Popcorn is an often overlooked, perfectly suitable appetizer. I have heard of a bar in Portland where they serve popcorn with truffle oil and one cook I know makes a mean caramelized shallot and blue cheese version. Anytime I have set out a bowl at a party or have been a guest at a party where there was popcorn it always goes fast!

When I was kid, my mom would make popcorn for us. We (my brothers, assorted neighborhood kids, myself) would sit around the breakfast nook in the kitchen and watch Mom at the stove. What she did which encouraged us all to watch closely was a bit of kitchen magic. First, she made a show of adding the oil and then 3 kernels of popcorn to the pot. Then, when we were being kids and easily distracted, she would add the rest of the popcorn and voila! She could make, as far as I could ever tell, a whole pot of popped popcorn from just 3 kernels. Incredible! Here is how I make what is called "girl" popcorn at our house. "Boy" popcorn of course has the more traditional butter and salt.

2 tbsp plain olive oil

½ c popcorn

EVOO

soy sauce or tamari

nutritional yeast powder

Pop the corn. Put it in a much larger bowl than the amount of popcorn you have. Drizzle with EVOO, soy sauce and sprinkle with nutritional yeast powder. Toss to mix. You now have "girl" popcorn. Put it in a pretty dish on the table and eat it up!

BREAKFAST

Breakfast Strata Sweet or Savory

Biscuits with Peppered Mushroom Gravy

Scones Sweet or Savory

Sweet Pumpkin Bread with Ginger

Summer Squash Bread

Hashbrowns

Fabulous Muffins (Cherry, Coconut, Carrot, Cinnamon)

Farmer's Skillet New Potatoes

Huevos Rancheros

French Toast

Banana Walnut Pancakes

Breakfast Strata, Sweet or Savory

9 servings

A friend of my Mother gave her a recipe written on a half sheet of paper which we called "Eggbake". The first ingredient was 8 slices white bread. When I started cooking at summer camp, I used this recipe and still called it eggbake when I served it to the campers and staff. It was a great help in using up the leftovers in a budget conscious kitchen at the end of a ten day camp session. The more I cooked, the more I read cookbooks and the more I learned about food and cooking. One thing I learned is that the eggbake I loved is also called strata. All of these kinds of recipes call for mixing everything together the night before and baking them in the morning. This allows the egg and milk mixture to soak up into the dry bread. Many recipes call for drying out the bread in the oven as a first step. Over the years, I have found myself tossing dried out heals from artisan loaves and toasted uneaten bits of baguettes into a bag in the freezer in anticipation of collecting enough for a strata. Doing so removes the need to dry bread out in the oven. Making the strata the night before is great if you are serving brunch, or do not mind waiting in the morning for the strata to come up to room temperature out of the refrigerator before baking for 55 minutes in the oven. I prefer to soak the dry bread in a little bit of water to facilitate the absorption of the milk and eggs. This step also allows you to mix and bake the strata all at once.

8 c sturdy dry bread cubes

1 c water

4 eggs

2 c milk

Toss the dry bread cubes with water in a large bowl and set aside. Stir occasionally while preparing the other ingredients. In a separate bowl, add the milk and eggs. Mix until uniform in consistency.

Sweet

1 ½ c fresh or frozen berries (blueberries, raspberries, blackberries etc.)

3 tbsp brown sugar

¼ tsp table salt

2 tsp turbinado sugar

In a mixing bowl, toss the berries with the brown sugar and table salt. Add the berry mixture to the bread cubes and mix. Add the milk and egg mixture. Pour into an 8x8 baking pan. Push down evenly with a spatula. Sprinkle with turbinado sugar. Bake in a 350 degree oven for 55 minutes. Serve warm.

Savory

8 oz bulk breakfast sausage or vegetarian breakfast sausage

2 c sliced crimini mushrooms

1 tbsp olive oil

1 bunch green onions

1 c cubed Swiss cheese (¼ " x ¼ ")

1 tsp kosher salt

¼ tsp fresh ground black pepper

In a fry pan on medium heat cook the bulk sausage breaking it into smaller bite size pieces as you go. Drain the fat and add the sausage to the bowl with the bread cubes and stir. In the same pan, heat the olive oil until it shimmers, then add the sliced mushrooms. Sauté until cooked through and add to the bowl with the sausage and bread cubes. Stir to mix. Add the chopped green onions, cubed Swiss cheese, salt and fresh ground pepper.

Stir the mixture. Add the milk and eggs and stir well again. Pour into an 8x8 baking pan. Push down evenly with a spatula. Bake in a 350 degree oven for 55 minutes. Serve warm.

Biscuits with Peppered Mushroom Gravy

4 servings

I love to eat biscuits and gravy. It is not often that I do because to make them at home takes some time and planning ahead. On the other hand to eat them at a breakfast restaurant, for me, means to find a breakfast restaurant which makes meat-free gravy. And so, when I do make biscuits and gravy, it is with planning and anticipation and they never fail to satisfy. There is always enough to eat for several days in a row.

Baking Powder Biscuits

makes approximately 16 2" biscuits

2 c flour

1 tbsp baking powder

½ tsp salt

¼ c butter

¼ c vegetable shortening

¾ c whole milk

Add the flour, baking powder and salt to a large mixing bowl and stir to mix. Cut the butter and shortening unto tablespoon-sized chunks and add to the dry ingredients. Using your fingers and working quickly, gently flatten the butter and shortening into pieces the size of pennies. Add the milk and stir until incorporated. The dough should be shaggy and a little sticky. Turn out onto a piece of parchment paper. Flatten the dough gently into a rectangle and fold it over onto itself. Flatten and fold the dough three more times and then pat out into a rectangle about half an inch thick. Use a sharp biscuit cutter to cut out the biscuits. Place them on an ungreased cookie sheet just about a finger width apart. Gently push the remaining dough together and cut out the rest of the biscuits.

Brush them with melted butter. Bake in a 450 degree oven for 10 – 12 minutes until nicely brown on top.

Peppered Mushroom Gravy

makes approximately 4 cups

4 c chopped crimini mushrooms

1 chopped medium yellow onion

3 tbsp butter

1 tsp salt

¼ c flour

3 c warm whole milk

1 tsp soy sauce

1 tsp salt

1 ½ tsp fresh ground black pepper

Optional: 2 drops liquid smoke

Chop the mushrooms and onions in a food processor until they are small uniform chunks. Heat a cast iron skillet to medium and add 2 tbsp of butter and 1 tsp of salt. Sauté the mushrooms and onions for about 7 minutes until very soft. Turn down the heat and add 1 more tablespoon of butter to the skillet. Once the butter has melted, add the flour and cook it in with the mushrooms and onions for 3 minutes, stirring constantly. Slowly add the warm milk ¼ c at a time. After each addition stir to incorporate and remove lumps. Once all of the milk has been added and the mixture has thickened, add the soy sauce, salt and fresh ground pepper. Taste and adjust the seasoning. Just before serving, add an extra teaspoon or two of fresh cracked pepper to the gravy.

Serve warm over hot-from-the-oven biscuits.

Scones, Sweet or Savory

16 scones

For me, the scone, along with biscotti, was one of the first accessible and yet seemingly exotic food treats. Both of these items were sold at various cafes near where I attended college. They were both inexpensive and both not part of the food culture I had grown up with at home. Even now, when I make scones or biscotti at home I feel transported to another country, and I like that feeling.

> 3 ½ c flour
>
> 3 tbsp sugar
>
> 2 tbsp baking powder
>
> ½ tsp table salt
>
> ¾ c butter (very cold)
>
> 2 eggs
>
> 1 c whole milk

In a large mixing bowl stir together the flour, sugar, baking powder and salt. Cut the butter into teaspoon-sized chunks and toss in the flour mixture. Using your fingers and working quickly flatten each piece of butter into a flake coated with flour. In a small mixing bowl, whisk the eggs and milk together. Pour the wet into the dry and stir with a fork until the dough comes together in a shaggy ball. Scrape all of the dough out onto a large piece of parchment paper and knead a few times. Flatten the dough out into a large rectangle. Spread one of the sets of ingredients below (savory scones or sweet scones) over the top of the dough.

<u>Savory Scones</u>

1c grated parmesan reggiano

2 tbsp dried basil

2 tsp kosher salt – for sprinkling on the finished scones

<u>Sweet Scones</u>

Zest of one large orange

1 c dried cranberries

1 tbsp turbinado sugar – for sprinkling on the finished scones

Fold one third of the dough in on itself and the last third up over the other two. Flatten back into a rectangle and fold this way again. This time, cut the dough in half and flatten it into two circles about 1 – 1 ½ inches thick. Cut each circle into 8 triangles. Space the scones evenly on a cookie sheet and brush with milk. Sprinkle the savory scones with kosher salt and the sweet scones with turbinado sugar. Bake in a 400 degrees oven for 18 minutes. These are also easy to freeze before cooking.

Sweet Pumpkin Bread with Ginger

One loaf

Sweet bread like banana, zucchini or this sweet pumpkin bread with ginger are a way for adults to eat cake for breakfast. I think this is very sneaky. These sweet styles of breads take much longer than muffins to cook in the morning. But they are so delicious that for me, they are worth the extra time and effort. Old bananas and the bounty of summer squash, produced by the home gardener every August, often become ingredients for these breads. It is the fall crop of pumpkins that take the extra effort to prepare. Yet they will store so well and keep you with a supply of this delicious bread all winter, to which this recipe is dedicated.

1 ¾ c flour

1 tsp baking soda

¼ tsp baking powder

½ tsp table salt

1 tsp Vietnamese cinnamon

1 ½ c sugar

½ c olive oil

2 eggs

1 ½ c Marina di Chioggia pumpkin puree (or substitute another pumpkin or canned pumpkin)

3 tbsp crystallized ginger chopped fine

2 tsp butter for loaf pan (substitute olive oil for a dairy free option)

In a large mixing bowl, whisk together the flour, baking soda, baking powder, salt and cinnamon. In a medium mixing bowl, whisk together the sugar, olive oil, eggs, pumpkin puree and crystallized ginger. Add the wet mixture to the dry mixture and stir until just completely uniform but no more. Grease a loaf pan with 2 teaspoons of butter. Spread the thick batter into the greased loaf pan and spread evenly. Bake in the middle of an oven at 350 degrees for 55-60 minutes. A toothpick inserted in the center should come out clean when finished. Cool on a wire rack before removing from the baking pan.

Summer Squash Bread

One loaf

If you have an abundance of summer squash, simply shred it and freeze it. It can be used at any time to make this bread or summer squash fritters (pg. 163). Next to banana bread, zucchini bread is probably the next most popular bread of this style. I myself like to use whatever variety of summer squash is on hand. By using both yellow and green squash summer squash varieties, you give the bread a confetti of color. In addition to the summer squash variety, I like to add an extra kick of cinnamon. With the prevalence of specialty spice stores these days, you can keep a good supply of a variety of cinnamons on hand to cook and bake with, which is such a treat.

2 c grated summer squash (any combination of cocozelle zucchini, Benning's green tint patty pan, crookneck, etc.)

3 eggs

1 ¼ c oil

1 ¼ c sugar

2 tsp vanilla extract

2 c flour

1 ½ tsp baking soda

1 tsp baking powder

1 tsp salt

2 ½ tsp Vietnamese cinnamon

2 tsp butter for loaf pan (substitute olive oil for a dairy free option)

Grate the summer squash and set aside. In a large bowl mix eggs, oil, sugar and vanilla until light in color. Fold in the summer squash. Sift the flour, baking soda, baking powder, salt and cinnamon onto the squash mixture and then stir to blend. Use butter to grease the loaf pan being thoroughly in the corners and seams. Pour batter into pan and put into a 350 degree oven for about 55-60 minutes. Bread is done when a toothpick inserted into the center comes out clean. Cool on a rack.

Hashbrowns

Serving size varies

Hash browns are tricky. For such a simple food (made from a single ingredient: potatoes) and preparation (fried in a pan with oil) it is amazing how often they can turn out to be a mushy, burned, half cooked, pasty mess. Here are a few tips I use to keep our hash browns crisp on the outside and cooked through on the inside. I prefer the standard russet potato when making hash browns.

The first order of business is to shred the potatoes into a bowl of cold water with a pinch of salt. When you have finished, swirl the potatoes around a bit and then drain them into a colander. This next part is key: toss your potatoes into a cotton kitchen towel, two handfuls at a time. Twist the towel closed and squeeze out any remaining excess water. Transfer to a dry bowl. Do this until all of the shredded potatoes have been squeezed dry. Next, heat a pan with plenty of oil. When the oil is hot, carefully sprinkle a layer of potatoes around the pan and squash them flat with a spatula. You should not be able to see the pan through the layer of potatoes but it should be less than one inch thick. Turn the heat down and put a lid on the pan allowing them to cook slowly and become crisp at the pan surface. After 8 – 10 minutes, remove the lid, loosen the potatoes with a spatula and then either toss them into the air to flip them over (a few flying shreds or a complete miss should not dissuade you from an attempt). A less risky method is to gently slide the whole mass crisp side down onto a plate. Then turn the frying pan upside down and place it over the potatoes on the plate, slide a hand under the plate and holding tightly to the handle of the frying pan, flip the whole contraption upside down, inverting the hash browns into the frying pan crisp side up. Add another splash of oil around the edge of the frying pan and swirl the inverted hash browns to distribute the oil. This time around, keep the lid off while cooking. Again, use low heat to cook the potatoes slowly without allowing them to burn. When the second side is sufficiently crisp, give them a sprinkle of salt and pepper, slide them on to a plate and eat them immediately with your favorite condiments. I prefer a little bit of sour cream and a splash of any available hot sauce.

Fabulous Muffins (Cherry Coconut Carrot Cinnamon)

10 muffins

Just before moving off of the farm, we were busy wrapping up the harvest season, putting the fields to bed for the winter, packing up the house and finishing off all the food stores in the pantry. One morning I wanted to make muffins and saw a few dried cherries and a quarter bag of coconut left in the pantry. I thought I would add them to my carrot muffins, which I prefer to dose with a hefty portion of cinnamon. Not only did these muffins look good bursting with carrots, cherries and coconut, but they tasted fabulous!

¾ c white flour

¼ c almond flour

1 tsp baking soda

2 tsp Vietnamese cinnamon

¼ tsp table salt

¼ c + t Tbsp olive oil

½ c sugar

1 egg

2 tbsp sour cream

2 tbsp milk (or water)

¾ c shredded Danvers carrot

¼ c shredded coconut

¼ c dried cherries

Mix the white four, almond flour, baking soda, salt, and cinnamon together in a bowl and set aside. In another bowl, whisk together the oil and sugar. Then add the egg and mix well. Lastly, add the sour cream and milk, and incorporate evenly. Gently fold the wet mixture into the dry mixture until just moistened through. Add the carrots, coconut and dried cherries and gently fold to distribute evenly. Fill paper lined muffin tins 2/3 full. Bake in a 350 degree oven for 18 minutes.

Farmer's Skillet New Potatoes

4 Servings

I had not known you could plant potatoes in your greenhouse in February and harvest them to eat in May. Our first year at the farmers market we saw one booth selling these young potatoes and our customers asked if we had any. The following February, we tucked a bunch of potato slips into the ground inside one of our green houses, covered them with straw and waited. In May, just after the market season started we dug up the rows and were rewarded with mounds of delicate skinned, tender new potatoes, bursting with flavor. If you can find these young uncured potatoes at your local farmers market in the spring or at first harvest in the fall, do not pass them up! I prefer to steam new potatoes and then either chill them for later use in salads or cube them up directly to sauté for a perfect spring "Farmer's Skillet".

2 ½ c steamed Bintje new potatoes cut into uniformed sized pieces

½ Walla Walla sweet onion diced

1 c crimini mushroom sliced thin

½ green pepper diced

3 eggs

½ c shredded cheddar cheese (optional)

kosher salt

fresh cracked black pepper

¼ c olive oil

Add 2 tablespoons olive oil to a pan and sauté the onion, mushrooms and peppers together with a pinch of salt until soft. Set the sautéed vegetables aside on a plate. Add 2 tablespoons olive oil to the pan and fry the potatoes until golden brown and crisp. Add the sautéed vegetables back to the pan and stir to distribute evenly among the potatoes. Crack the eggs into a bowl and whisk lightly. Turn the heat down to the lowest setting and add the eggs to the golden brown potatoes and sautéed vegetables. Shake the pan to distribute the eggs evenly. Put a lid on the pan to cook the eggs all the way through without stirring. When the eggs have set on the top, remove the pan from the heat. Evenly sprinkle the cheese over the top and put the lid back on to melt the cheese. When the cheese has melted sprinkle everything with a pinch of salt and fresh cracked pepper. Serve warm.

Huevos Rancheros

2 servings

A friend from New Zealand once said to me "What is it with you Americans and Mexican food?" I do not exactly know, but I do find Mexican food delicious, in addition to most fusion variations which have been cooked up this side of the border. One of my favorite dishes, which I have eaten often enough to go so far as saying it is comfort food for me, is huevos rancheros. This dish is both simple and satisfying. On the farm, we produced many of the ingredients for this dish: eggs from the chickens, black beans, tomatoes, onions and peppers from the gardens. When making huevos rancheros at home, I like to spread the beans over the tortillas, make a well in the center and gently poach the eggs under cover with a little water added to the pan for steam.

Pico de Gallo (pg. 10)

1 ½ c Black Turtle beans, cooked

1 ½ tsp ground cumin

½ tsp granulated garlic

½ tsp smoked paprika

1 ½ tbsp soy sauce (substitute tamari for a gluten free option)

1/3 c water

8 corn tortillas

4 eggs

1 avocado

¼ c sour cream (optional)

fresh cilantro

Add the black beans, seasonings, soy sauce and water to a small pot. Bring to a simmer and gently smash the beans in the pot. Check for seasoning. Simmer until thick and then remove from heat and set aside. In a large skillet gently warm pairs of tortillas side by side. Turn over several times to warm through. Divide the beans equally among the four pairs of tortillas by mounding them in the center of each pair. Spread the beans out making a shallow well in the center. Crack an egg into each well. Pour 1/3 c water around the edge of the skillet in between the tortillas and put a lid on the skillet. Gently steam the eggs on medium heat for about 10 minutes. Check after 5 minutes and add more water if necessary. Remove the tortillas from the pan and slide onto individual serving plates. Garnish with pico de gallo, slices of avocado, sour cream and fresh chopped cilantro. Olé!

French Toast

2 servings

While living in Japan, this was one of the familiar foods we could replicate without searching high and low for ingredients. And it is worth pointing out the extreme importance of having at least one familiar food that you can replicate while living overseas without much trouble! When making French toast, I personally prefer to dry the slices out overnight. It takes little time after dinner to slice up any leftover bread and leave it to dry out overnight on the counter.

½ of a narrow baguette sliced ½" thick

¾ c plain yogurt

2 tsp sugar

pinch of table salt

1 egg

butter

jam and or maple syrup

Mix the yogurt, sugar, salt and egg well with a whip. The ending mixture should be rather goopy. Heat up a fry pan and melt 1-2 tablespoons of butter. Start on medium temperature for your stove and adjust up or down as necessary to cook battered bread slowly. Dip pieces of bread into the egg mixture and coat on both sides. Place into the fry pan. Cover with a lid or piece of foil and allow it to cook until the top is almost dry and the bottom is nicely browned, about 3 minutes. Turn each piece over and allow the brown on the opposite side. When finished, remove from pan and serve immediately with jam or maple syrup.

Banana Walnut Pancakes

18 - 3" pancakes

Years ago when I cooked at summer camp, pancake breakfast was a celebration of color. I do not remember now who in the kitchen thought our pancakes should be the colors of the rainbow, but I do remember supporting the activity. Camp session after camp session we would wake up one morning to make gallons and gallons of pancake mix, pour it into individual plastic juice pitchers, and with little tiny plastic bottles of food coloring, we would turn the batter into a rainbow. Our summer campers would actually send their camp counselor back to the kitchen to request certain colors for seconds. These days, my favorite pancakes are sourdough, which take a little planning ahead. One morning, craving pancakes but with no sourdough to use, I spied a very ripe banana in the fruit bowl. The idea for banana walnut pancakes sprang into my head and has been worthy of many repeats ever since. Enjoy!

1 c flour

1 tsp baking powder

¼ tsp baking soda

¼ tsp table salt

1 c buttermilk

1 smashed banana

2 tbsp olive oil

1 egg

¼ c finely ground walnuts

Mix the flour, baking powder, baking soda and salt together in a bowl and make a well in the center. In another bowl mix the buttermilk, banana, olive oil and egg. Pour the wet mixture into the well and mix until incorporated. Fold in the smashed up walnuts.

Cook in a cast iron skillet on medium heat. Turn when bubbles just start to form on the upper side of the pancakes. Pancakes will puff up in the middle when finished cooking. Serve warm with butter and syrup.

SALAD DRESSINGS

Sweet Pesto Dressing

Farm Ranch Dressing

Chipotle Mayo

Thousand Island or Fry Sauce

Japanese Citrus Dressing

Miso Dressing

Classic Vinaigrette

Sweet Pesto Dressing

Makes approximately 1 cup

One year while I was in college, I shared a big, open craftsman style house with a number of friends - one whose father owned and operated the local winery. Annually at this winery, they would hold a dinner in the main cellar for all of their case buyers. All of us at the house would go out to the winery on this dinner weekend and help wash up all the dishes in the back room. The caterer was so friendly, and along with his wife, would come every year to produce the dinner. He always served a sweet pesto dressing on the salad. When I tasted this dressing for the first time, I was blown away at the dressing's perfect flavor. For years, I tried to re-create it in my own kitchen without success. Until, I was introduced to sweetened rice wine vinegar. This is so easy and so good.

> 6 tbsp pesto (homemade or from a jar)
>
> ½ c + 1 tbsp seasoned rice wine vinegar
>
> Pinch of table salt to taste

Whisk all of the ingredients together in a small bowl.

Farm Ranch Dressing

Makes approximately 1 cup

I love ranch dressing and have been accused at times of eating more of it than I should. In the grocery store, there is a really shocking amount of space dedicated to salad dressing. This when you consider the ease of making your own dressing at home in such a quick amount of time, with ingredients you have on hand. "Ranch" style itself is one of several popular dressings with repeated variations across brands and price points. Here is my homemade version which has a bright and clean flavor. It is perfectly suitable for making and using immediately, but does, as with some things, taste better the following day.

½ c mayonnaise

½ c plain yogurt

1 tsp dried basil

½ tsp granulated garlic

½ tsp table salt

½ tsp fresh ground black pepper

Pinch of finely ground white pepper

Whisk all of the ingredients together in a small bowl. Let rest at least thirty minutes before serving, for the flavors to blend.

Chipotle Mayo

Makes approximately ¾ cup

Chipotle is a flavor that was not a part of my childhood. I do not recall the first time I tasted these smokey peppers in adobo sauce, but it must have been on one of my first trips to Baja, Mexico during college. I do remember purchasing tiny little cans of chipotle peppers in adobo sauce at the "tienda" during my travels to bring home. Back then, my favorite thing to do was toast up a sesame seed bagel (from the best bagel shop I have ever visited, in downtown Bellingham, Washington), smear it with plain cream cheese and then a mouth-on-fire spoonful of chopped chipotle in adobo sauce. Now at least on the west coast, where I have spent all my time and done all my food shopping, it is not hard to find either a can of chipotle chilies or a bottle of chipotle hot sauce in the local supermarket. This chipotle mayo is perfect as a sandwich spread or dipping sauce for sweet potato and regular french fries. It can also be thinned with cream, milk or water for a terrific salad or coleslaw dressing.

½ c mayonnaise

1 tbsp water

1 chopped chipotle pepper in adobo sauce

(or 2 tbsp bottled chipotle pepper sauce)

Whisk all of the ingredients together in a small bowl.

Thousand Island Dressing or Fry Sauce

Makes approximately 1 ¼ cup

I have been making this dressing from scratch longer than any other. It goes back to my time cooking at a summer camp the year I turned sixteen. Starting out as a dishwasher, I for some reason, thought nothing of volunteering to be the assistant cook to the assistant who thought nothing of volunteering to be the head cook when the head cook left suddenly after the first week. We were getting ourselves into cooking three meals a day, ten days on two days off, for 50-70 staff and campers. In addition, as this camp was for special needs individuals, there were a number of special diets which needed attention. We managed to not only keep everyone fed, but with no real adult supervision, we had a really magnificent amount of fun in the kitchen. Of course, we put burgers on the menu every session, and fries and fry sauce go with burgers. And I always thought thousand island dressing looked and tasted like fry sauce. Here is how we made it then and how I still like it now.

- 1/2 c mayonnaise
- 3 tbsp ketchup
- 2 tbsp chopped dill pickle
- 2 tbsp chopped white onion
- ½ tsp celery salt
- ½ tsp granulated garlic
- ½ tsp fresh ground black pepper

Place all of the ingredients together in a small bowl. Use an immersion blender to puree everything together.

Japanese Citrus Dressing

Makes approximately ½ cup

"Ponzu" is most certainly not a North American flavor. However, it is decidedly delicious and worth the effort to pursue a bottle of ponzu if you are fond of citrus flavors. You can usually find at least one brand available in the Asian food section of a large grocery store. The base flavor and component is soy sauce, but other ingredients give it a complex savory citrus taste. More expensive varieties contain the juice of yuzu and or sudachi citrus fruits.

3 tbsp Ponzu (Japanese soy sauce and citrus; if not available, substitute ½ soy sauce and ½ lemon, lime or orange juice)

5 tbsp mayonnaise

½ tsp fresh cracked pepper

1 tbsp water

Whisk all of the ingredients together in a small bowl.

Miso Dressing

Makes approximately 1 cup

"Miso" is a fermented paste made primarily of soy beans, although some variations include other ingredients. Until living and working in Japan, I never thought of miso as anything other than a soup. It does, make a wonderful topping for steamed or broiled fish, a dip for vegetables, a brine for making pickles, and wonderful salad dressing. Quick and delicious dressing can be made of any miso flavor, although some adjustment for sweet and salty is necessary depending upon which variety of miso paste you start with in your kitchen.

6 tbsp miso paste

¼ c olive oil

1/2 c seasoned rice wine vinegar

1/2 tsp finely ground black pepper

4 tsp honey

2 tbsp water

Whisk all of the ingredients together in a small bowl. Taste and adjust for seasoning.

Variations:

Add 2 tbsp finely chopped green onion

Add 2 tsp toasted sesame seeds

Classic Vinaigrette

Makes approximately ½ cup

A classic: This is how I like to make it at home in my kitchen.

- 5 tbsp EVOO
- 2 tbsp red wine vinegar
- 1 clove garlic
- 2 tsp Dijon mustard
- ¼ tsp kosher salt
- ½ tsp fresh cracked pepper

Peel and crush the garlic clove through a garlic press into a small mixing bowl. Stir in the salt. Add the remaining ingredients and whisk them all together. Taste and adjust for seasoning.

SALADS

Arugula Parmesan

Coleslaw with Variations

Tuscan Kale Salad

Little Gems with Strawberries

Mizuna & Tofu Salad

Speckled Amish Bibb with Goat Cheese & Raspberries

Iceberg Wedge Salad

Panzanella

Spinach Salad

Corn Salad

Greek Salad

Arugula Parmesan

4 servings

This salad rivals the iceberg wedge in its spectacular simplicity. It is good when offered as the "green side salad" at restaurant after restaurant in New Zealand and Australia. It is very good when the arugula is fresh from your own garden, or recently harvested and purchased from a local farmer at a market. It moves to spectacularly delicious when the aged balsamic vinegar is ancient, thick and sweet and the grated parmesan is of the highest quality.

    4 c loosely packed Arugula (or rocket)

    ½ c freshly grated parmesan reggiano

    ½ c aged balsamic vinegar*

    Maldon sea salt

Evenly distribute the greens onto four salad plates. Drizzle each plate with 2 tbsp of the aged balsamic vinegar. Sprinkle 2 tbsp of freshly grated parmesan reggiano over each salad. Finish by tossing a few crystals of the Maldon salt over each salad and serve.

*plain balsamic vinegar will not substitute unless you first reduce the volume of liquid slowly without scorching, in a sauce pan and then cool to room temperature

Coleslaw with Variations

For a long time, my favorite way to eat coleslaw was on top of a big slice of cornbread and underneath a piece of grilled salmon - sort of a coleslaw sandwich if you will. I know there are folks who might cringe at this style of mixing food but I am a big fan of everything in one bowl for dinner. This coleslaw I used to make also had, as one secret ingredient, raisins. The other was a packet of powdered dressing mix. Folks loved it. Below are a couple of slightly more refined variations of coleslaw, both of which I would eat as noted above!

Coleslaw with Arugula

4 servings

The addition of arugula to this salad gives it a peppery punch that makes your taste buds wake up and say "AHH". Try it as a side dish with barbecue chicken, salmon or ribs.

2 c shredded Early Jersey Wakefield cabbage

1 c chopped Arugula (or rocket)

¼ tsp salt

½ tsp finely ground black pepper

1 tbsp red wine vinegar

2 tbsp mayonnaise

Coleslaw with Cilantro and Lime

4 servings

This salad is excellent with fish tacos, quesadillas and enchiladas. The lime and cilantro ramp up the flavor punch.

- 4 c shredded Early Jersey Wakefield cabbage
- ¼ c white onion
- ¼ c cilantro
- ½ lime
- ¼ tsp salt
- ¼ tsp pepper
- 3 tbsp mayonnaise

In a large mixing bowl, add the cabbage, finely diced white onion and chopped cilantro. Squeeze the lime over the vegetables. Add the salt, pepper and mayonnaise. Stir to mix completely. Let rest for 10 minutes. Stir again before serving.

Tuscan Kale Salad

6 servings

This salad came to us by way of one of our best market customers. She described it one day when purchasing a bunch of Tuscan kale. I went home, made the salad, and fell in love. Later in the summer, when our three nieces were visiting, I made the salad for dinner one night. Not only did they eat it all, but it was requested for dinner again the next night. Never in my wildest dreams growing up did I ever request kale. And here was a kale salad so good to eat, it was requested by kids! Needless to say I was happy to oblige.

> 8 oz Tuscan kale (Dinosaur, Nero di Toscana, Lacinato)
>
> ½ c panko
>
> 2 tbsp EVOO
>
> ½ tsp kosher Salt
>
> 2 tsp fresh ground black pepper
>
> ½ c freshly grated parmesan reggiano
>
> ½ lemon juiced
>
> ½ lime Juice

Using a sharp knife, carefully cut the ribs out of the kale. Wash, dry and chiffonade the kale leaves. Toss them into a large mixing bowl along with the remaining ingredients. Mix thoroughly, then press the salad down fully into the bowl and set it aside in the fridge for several hours or overnight to marinate. Mix well again prior to serving.

Little Gems with Strawberries

4 servings

This is a very quick and easy lunch salad to make after a morning spent shopping at your local farmers market. "Little gems" are not only the cutest little heads of lettuce I have ever grown but also the tenderest. One head sliced in half, per person, is perfect for a lovely salad.

4 heads of Little Gem lettuce (substitute any tender delicate green butter lettuce – the smaller the better)

1 c sliced fresh strawberries

¼ c EVOO

2 tbsp strawberry jam

1 ½ tbsp champagne vinegar

pinch kosher salt

fresh cracked pepper

Carefully rinse each head of little gem lettuce and trim the bottom core away. Cut each head in half and set decoratively on a plate. Distribute the fresh sliced strawberries over each plate of lettuce. In a small bowl whisk together the EVOO, strawberry jam, champagne vinegar and pinch of kosher salt. Dress the salads at the last minute. Grind some fresh pepper over each salad and serve.

Mizuna & Tofu Salad

4 servings

Peppery, tender, young "mizuna" is such a good salad green first thing in the spring. I loved to eat mizuna in all of its useful ways while we lived in Japan. Salads of course, but also simmered in hearty winter soups, sautéed in stir-frys or added to fried rice. Back in the States, on the farm we grew mizuna and added mizuna pesto (pg. 12) and this delicious salad to the ways we like to eat this versatile mustard green.

    1 bunch tender young Mizuna

    1 bunch French breakfast radishes

    1 brick firm tofu

    1 recipe Japanese Citrus Dressing (pg. 57)

    fresh cracked black pepper

Rinse and chop the mizuna into 2" pieces and place them in the bottom of the salad bowls. Slice the radishes and sprinkle them over the top of the mizuna. Drain the tofu in a colander. Wrap the tofu in a clean kitchen towel and carefully squeeze out more of the liquid without breaking apart the tofu. Cut the drained and dried tofu into ½" cubes and distribute them evenly over the radishes. Drizzle the dressing over each salad. Add fresh cracked pepper before serving.

Speckled Amish Bibb with Goat Cheese & Raspberries

4 servings

"Speckled Amish Bibb" is a delicate heirloom head lettuce. As its name suggests, it is covered with rouge-colored speckles. We once had a lady return to the market the weekend after purchasing of a bag of tender young Speckled Amish Bibb leaves to tell us she had thrown out the lettuce because it had spots! After that we were sure to indicate to all of our new customers that our lettuce was supposed to have speckles.

1 head Speckled Amish Bibb (or other very tender bibb lettuce)

½ pint fresh raspberries

4 oz chevre (goat cheese)

¼ c EVOO

2 tbsp red wine vinegar

1 tsp kosher salt

fresh cracked pepper

Tear lettuce into bite-sized pieces and wash and dry in a salad spinner. In a small colander rinse the raspberries and gently shake dry. Slice the chevre into four even pieces. Start building the salads in four bowls by evenly distributing the lettuce. Add a slice of chevre in the center of the bowl on top of the lettuce. Evenly drizzle the EVOO over each bowl and sprinkle with vinegar. Add a pinch of salt over each salad and also the fresh cracked pepper (with a heavy dose right onto the chevre). Finally, evenly distribute the raspberries around each salad. Serve with EVOO and vinegar at the table to taste.

Iceberg Wedge Salad

6 servings

I have been to a steak house which claimed to have the "World's finest iceberg wedge" salad. It was not. It was a wedge of iceberg lettuce drowning in a puddle of dressing with olives, white onion slices and tomatoes. It was a salad to be sure, but what makes the iceberg wedge salad so magnificent is the simple preparation, and the perfect flavor and texture combination. Lettuce, blue cheese dressing and wafer thin slices of red onion - that's it. Try it for yourself.

1 head iceberg lettuce cut into 6 wedges (very cold)

1 ½ c blue cheese dressing

¾ c blue cheese crumbles

1 Rossa di Milano purple onion sliced wafer thin (or other purple globe onion)

Plate each wedge onto a salad plate. Drizzle each wedge with ¼ c of blue cheese dressing. Divide the onion slices equally over the six wedges. Sprinkle two tablespoons of blue cheese crumbles over each salad. Serve immediately.

Panzanella

4 servings

This is one of my all time favorite salads. It is a perfect combination of beautiful-to-look-at and delicious-to-eat. The salad is substantial enough to be eaten as an entrée if you should like to do so. While living in Japan, panzanella was the first non-Japanese style salad I made. And it took a special trip across town to the 'foreign' food store in the mall to find pine nuts, dried cranberries and parmesan cheese. Later, as I became familiar with reading Japanese and the layout of the Japanese grocery store, I was able to locate more 'foreign' ingredients in my local stores without a special trip across town.

1 head Black Seeded Simpson green leaf lettuce

1 small Walla Walla sweet yellow onion

3 tbsp pine nuts

3 tbsp dried cranberries

10 Red Pear tomatoes (or other red mini tomato)

¼ cup parmesan reggiano

2 c sturdy dry French bread cubes or chunks

3 tbsp butter

1 tsp salt

1 tsp dried basil

1 tsp granulated garlic

½ c EVOO

¼ c red wine vinegar

fresh cracked pepper

Shred the lettuce into bite size pieces. Wash, dry and set aside.

Slice the onion in half and then from pole to pole in half moons. Sauté the onions in a pan with olive oil and a pinch of salt on medium heat until they are soft and start to brown. Add the sugar and stir constantly until it has melted and a nice uniform caramelized brown color is obtained. Remove from the heat, and place the onions in a dish into the refrigerator to cool.

Put the pine nuts in a fry pan on medium heat. Stir them constantly until they are golden brown in color. Remove from the heat and place the pine nuts into a dish set in the refrigerator to cool.

Slice French bread into cubes ½ x ½" or break into chunks. Melt the butter in fry pan on medium heat. Stir in the dried basil, half of the salt and granulated garlic. Add the French bread cubes and stir constantly until toasted. Transfer to a dish and place in the fridge to cool.

Shred the parmesan reggiano on the fat holes in the shredder for this salad.

Slice all mini tomatoes in half.

In a small bowl whisk the extra virgin olive oil and the red wine vinegar together.

Place the bread cubes in a large bowl and toss with ¼ c of the dressing. Add the lettuce, cranberries, pine nuts, tomatoes, onions and parmesan reggiano (reserve 2 tbsp.). Toss again to mix and add more dressing to taste. Top the salad with fresh cracked pepper and the remaining parmesan cheese.

Spinach Salad

4 servings

I once made this salad for an eighty-year-old Japanese lady who was astounded that you could eat spinach raw. I was astounded that was even a question. After I reassured her that in fact, you could eat spinach raw she did dig in and enjoy her salad. I hope you enjoy it as well.

one bunch spinach

½ Rossa di Milano purple onion (or other purple globe onion)

3 tbsp toasted almonds

3 tbsp dried cranberries

¼ c seasoned rice wine vinegar

2 tbsp extra virgin olive oil

fresh cracked black pepper

kosher salt

blue cheese (optional)

Slice the onion into ½ rings and place in a shallow dish with enough rice wine vinegar to just cover them up. Chop and wash the spinach and place it into a large salad bowl. Chop the almonds and add them to the spinach. Add the cranberries. When the onions are limp, remove them from the vinegar and add them to the bowl of other ingredients. Reserve the vinegar (which now has a light pink color and also onion flavor) and add a dash of pepper, salt, and the olive oil. Mix well with a fork. Drizzle over the salad ingredients in the bowl and toss well. Plate the salad for individual servings and sprinkle with crumbled blue cheese.

Corn Salad

6 servings

On one night of the week, the dinner menu at my first cooking job in Alaska was a robust Mexican theme which included a complimentary Corona for all the guests, and a corn salad. We used to talk about how great it would be if, in the off season, we could all just move to a sister lodge in Baja and keep on cooking. Twenty years later, we still do not have a sister lodge in Baja, but I still make corn salad.

4 c corn (frozen and thawed or fresh cooked off the cob)

2 Evergreen Hardy White scallions (or other green onions)

½ green pepper

1/2 c red pear tomatoes halved (or other red mini tomato)

1 sm can sliced black olives

¼ c chopped fresh cilantro

1 tsp kosher salt

½ tsp fresh cracked black pepper

juice of one lime

2 tbsp apple cider vinegar

2 tbsp sugar

1 tbsp olive oil

Put the corn into a large mixing bowl. Chop the scallions and add them to the bowl. Remove the seeds and ribs from half of a green pepper and cut it into small pea-sized pieces and add them to the bowl with the corn and green onions. Halve the cherry tomatoes and add them to the bowl with the other vegetables. Drain the sliced black olives and add them to the rest of the ingredients as well. To make the dressing, place the salt, pepper, lime juice, apple cider vinegar, sugar and olive oil in a small mixing bowl and whisk them together. Pour this over the vegetables in the large bowl and mix well. Rinse the cilantro and remove most of the stems. Roughly chop the cilantro and fold all but one tablespoon into the salad. Garnish the salad before serving with the remaining tablespoon of cilantro.

Greek Salad

6 servings

A friend in college used to make this salad. I found it to be quite different than the Greek salads that I have ordered on occasion in restaurants, which always seem to start with lettuce. This salad skips the lettuce altogether and is beautiful and delicious. It is a very straightforward dish but does taste better after resting for several hours.

1 large beefsteak tomato (such as Brandywine, Cherokee Purple or Moskvich)

1 green pepper

½ Rossa di Milano purple onion (or other purple globe onion)

1 English cucumber

½ c kalamata olives, whole pitted

¼ tsp kosher salt

½ tsp fresh cracked pepper

3 tbsp red wine vinegar

1 tbsp EVOO

4 oz feta cheese (made with sheep or goats milk)

Peel and cut the onion into large bite-sized chunks. Break the chunks of onion into individual pieces and soak in a bowl of cold water while preparing the other ingredients. Wash and seed the tomato, green pepper and cucumber. Cut all into bite-sized chunks and toss to mix them in a large mixing bowl. Drain the onions, pat them dry and add them to the other vegetables in the mixing bowl. Add the kalamata olives, salt, pepper, red wine vinegar, and EVOO. Toss well. Cut the feta cheese into kalamata olive-sized pieces and gently fold them into the salad. Let it rest for at least an hour before eating, or even overnight.

SOUPS AND SANDWICHES

Lentil Stew with Parsley Dumplings

White Star Farms' Gazpacho

Cream of Celery with Havarti

Two Bean Chili

Red Rhubarb Chard Quesadillas

Arugula Chicken Salad on Ciabatta

Bratwurst with Roasted Onion and Sauerkraut Relish on Hoagie Rolls

Three Cheese with Chips on Whole Wheat Toast

Wilted Spinach Croissant

Tofu Sliders with Wasabi Mayonnaise

Lentil Stew with Parsley Dumplings

Makes approximately 8 cups

I made this soup weekly for a couple of years during college. Back then if I was careful about what I bought, $50 a week could cover my groceries. On Sundays, while studying for the up and coming week, I would set this soup to boil and simmer away on the stove. What surprised me was coming around the corner of the kitchen one day to find my roommates eating the soup out of the pot with spoons. "We're sorry, but it is just so good!" they said. It had never occurred to me to make or serve this soup to anyone else. It was just an affordable and filling meal for me. After all these years, I do still make this soup, I do still like to eat it, and I have served it up a time or two to other folks.

2 medium Danvers carrots

1 medium yellow onion

2 c lentils

1 pint home canned whole peeled tomatoes (or 14 oz can whole peeled tomatoes)

1 ½ kosher salt

½ tsp granulated garlic

1 tsp paprika

3 tbsp soy sauce

1 tsp nutritional yeast powder

Dumplings

1 ¼ c flour

1 ½ tsp baking powder

1 tsp table salt

1 tsp freshly ground black pepper

2 tbsp butter

2 tbsp fresh Italian parsley

¾ c ½ and ½

2 tbsp EVOO

Maldon salt for finishing

Peel and chop the carrots and onions into bite-sized pieces. Add these to a large soup pot along with the lentils, tomatoes and seasoning (kosher salt, granulated garlic, paprika, soy sauce, nutritional yeast powder). Cover all with water and add 2 more cups. Bring to a boil then put the lid on the pot and simmer for 20 minutes, or until the lentils are cooked through, stirring occasionally.

When the lentils and vegetables have finished cooking and are seasoned to your satisfaction, make the dumplings. In a medium mixing bowl stir together the flour, baking powder, salt, and pepper for the dumplings. Add the cold butter and, using your hands, flatten out the pieces. While doing so, allow the butter to be coated with flour. Then gently mix and distribute the flattened pieces of butter through the dry mix. Add the parsley and mix gently until it has been evenly distributed. Pour in the ½ and ½ and stir until just moistened.

Drizzle 2 tablespoons of EVOO over the gently boiling soup in a pot. Tear off small pieces of the stiff dumpling dough and drop them evenly over the pot of soup. Place the lid on the pot and allow the dumplings to steam for 6 minutes.

When serving in a bowl, drizzle a bit of EVOO onto the top of the soup and sprinkle with a pinch of Maldon salt.

White Star Farms' Gazpacho

4 servings

When it was broiling hot outside while we were working on the farm, the very last thing we wanted to do was go inside and heat anything up for lunch. This quick gazpacho was a lifesaver on those hot summer days. It provided salt, hydration, flavor and I have to say, it was a very pretty dish to look at during lunch.

- 1 small green pepper
- 1 large beefsteak tomato (such as Brandywine, Cherokee Purple or Moskvich)
- 1 bunch Evergreen Hardy White scallions
- 2 tbsp extra EVOO
- 1 tsp lemon juice
- 1/2 tsp kosher salt
- 1/4 tsp fresh cracked pepper
- 4 medium cucumbers peeled and seeded
- 1/2 c water
- 1 tsp lemon juice
- 1/4 c sour cream
- table salt to taste

Chop the green pepper, tomato and scallions into small, pea-sized pieces. Add these together with the EVOO, lemon juice, salt and black pepper. Stir and let rest while you prepare the cucumbers.

Toss the peeled and seeded cucumbers into a food processor along with water, lemon juice and sour cream. Pulse until a fine puree is reached. Add salt to taste. To chill, nest a small bowl with the cucumber puree in it, into a larger bowl with a layer of ice cubes. Stir occasionally for 5 minutes or so until chilled.

Serve the cucumber puree in a bowl with a large spoonful of the pepper/tomato/onion relish and a dollop of real sour cream. Ahh, delightful!

Cream of Celery with Havarti

Makes approximately 8 cups

Whenever my mom and dad came to visit at the farm, mom would fill a cooler with items from their fridge at home, which she did not want spoiling while they were gone. Inevitably, she would bring a whole head of celery. And it would lie at the back of our fridge untouched until they departed. At that time; I would remember it was there, drag it out with a smile and make a big pot of this delicious soup. The smoked salt is for finishing. I am partial to alder smoked, but if you have a chance to taste-test smoked salts side by side, you should do so and then pick your own favorite.

- 3 c celery diced (~9 large ribs)
- 1 c yellow onion diced
- 2 tbsp olive oil
- 2 tbsp vermouth or white wine
- 2 tbsp butter
- 3 tbsp flour
- 2 c milk (warm)
- 2 c vegetable broth
- 1 tsp celery salt
- 1 tbsp soy sauce
- ¼ tsp white pepper
- 4 oz havarti cut into small cubes
- ¼ tsp smoked alder salt

Add the olive oil to a large heavy bottomed pot and heat until it starts to shimmer. Put the diced celery and onion into the pot and stir frequently until soft (about 15 minutes). Add the vermouth to the pan and scrape free any browned bits stuck to the bottom and sides of the pot as the vermouth is reduced by half. Add the butter. Once the butter has melted and the foaming subsides, add the flour. Stir constantly for two minutes. Slowly add the warm milk ½ cups at a time stirring all the while to incorporate without lumps. Then add the vegetable broth and seasonings. Stir over medium heat until the soup thickens. Add the cheese and stir until fully incorporated. Turn off the heat and allow to cool. Use an immersion blender to puree the soup. Test for correct seasoning and adjust if necessary. Serve drizzled with EVOO, fresh diced tomato and a sprinkle of smoked alder salt.

Two Bean Chili

Makes approximately 8 cups

I prefer buying dry beans and cooking them at home to purchasing beans in a can. A crock pot is my kitchen tool of choice for cooking beans. One overnight soak and one day in the crock pot gives you a good supply of beans, ready for any recipe of your choice. Cooked beans can be portioned out and stored in your freezer for quick use anytime. When making chili, I add all of the ingredients to the crock pot and let it cook away all day. Make a quick cornbread when you get home, and there is a perfectly delicious meal ready to go.

2 c dried pinto beans

2 c dried small red kidney beans

1 qt home canned whole peeled tomatoes (or 1 - 28 oz can of whole peeled tomatoes)

2 tsp celery salt

2 tsp granulated garlic

1 tsp finely ground black pepper

1 tbsp smoked paprika

2 tsp ground cumin

2 tsp cocoa powder

2 bay leaves

pinch ground chili pepper to taste (optional)

1 white onion

1 tsp kosher salt

2 tbsp olive oil

sour cream

cheddar cheese (shredded)

Put the four cups of beans into an 8 cup container. Rinse the beans and then fill the container of water up to 8 cups. Put a lid or some covering over the beans and water and set aside for the night. In the morning drain the beans. Place the beans, tomatoes, celery salt, granulated garlic, black pepper, paprika, cumin, cocoa powder, bay leaves and ground chili pepper into your crock pot. Add enough water to cover everything by two inches. Set the crock pot to slow cook for the day.

At any time you can grill the onions. If you do not have a grill, or time to grill them, you can cook them in the oven as noted here. Pre-heat the oven to 450 degrees. Set the top oven rack about 8" below the broiler. Cut the onion into 8ths and place in a mixing bowl. Add the salt and olive oil. Stir until coated. Place on a sheet pan and spread out evenly. Set on the top rack of the oven. Check after 10 minutes. When the onions have softened and started to brown, turn on the broiler. Keep a careful eye on the onions when the broiler is on. You should pull the onions from the oven when they are starting to brown all over, but before they burn. Some onions will be more browned than others. Add the onions and any scraped-up browned bits to the chili in the crock pot.

When the crock pot is finished, taste the chili and adjust for seasoning. Using an immersion blender, give the chili a couple of whirs to thicken up the 'sauce' and break up some of the larger tomato pieces. Serve with optional toppings of sour cream and cheddar cheese and a side of your favorite cornbread with cheddar and jalapenos (pg. 108).

Red Rhubarb Chard Quesadillas

4 servings

I had no concept of exactly how many tortillas I ate until moving to Japan when I suddenly did not have a single tortilla on hand. It was a funny wake-up call in the kitchen. You can tuck any kind of leftover in a tortilla and call it a meal, and it had become a go-to lunchtime treat for years while working summer seasonal jobs. It is also quick to make and eat. On the farm, more often than not, lunchtime consisted of one stuffed quesadilla or another. Here is one of our favorites.

8 corn tortillas

1 bunch Red Rhubarb chard (or other Swiss chard)

1 c Monterey jack cheese shredded

1 c Black Turtle beans

3 green Evergreen Hardy White scallions sliced

1 avocado

hot sauce (your favorite!)

olive oil for cooking

salt to taste

fry pan with a lid (large enough to accommodate two corn tortillas side by side)

Wash and tear the chard into bite-sized pieces. Lay the tortillas out on the counter or on a baking sheet. Add 2 tbsp cheese, 2 tbsp black beans, a sprinkling of green onions and a handful of chard to each tortilla. Heat 1 tbsp of oil in fry pan on medium high. Carefully place two loaded tortillas side by side in the fry pan. Place the lid on the fry pan and leave in place until the chard has wilted. Check often after 2 minutes for wilting and adjust heat if corn tortillas are getting to crisp. When the chard is wilted and the cheese has melted, turn out onto a plate; add hot sauce and salt to taste, and fold closed. Garnish with sliced of fresh ripe avocado. Ay ay aiy!

Arugula Chicken Salad on Ciabatta

4 sandwiches

This sandwich came about one day because this is what I had on hand in the fridge at lunchtime. There was leftover roasted chicken, a bag of arugula from the garden, fresh shallots and a little piece of gorgonzola left over from making pasta. I always like to keep a couple of nice rolls on hand in the freezer for last minute sandwich making and on this day, they were ciabatta rolls, which were perfect. This salad can be chopped up and stirred together quick as a wink and it is delicious.

4 ciabatta rolls

1 ½ c boneless cooked chicken

3 c lightly packed Arugula (or rocket)

1 shallot (half the size of a golf ball)

2 tbsp mayonnaise

1 tbsp plain yogurt

3 tbsp gorgonzola cheese crumbled

fresh cracked pepper

kosher salt

1 large beefsteak tomato (such as Brandywine, Cherokee Purple)

Dice the chicken and the shallot and add to a small mixing bowl. Chiffonade the arugula and add to the chicken mixture. In another small bowl, mix the mayonnaise, yogurt and gorgonzola cheese. Add salt and pepper to taste. Mix the dressing into the chicken mixture stirring well to coat with the dressing. Spread the salad onto each ciabatta roll and add thick slices of tomato. Enjoy!

Bratwurst with Roasted Onion and Sauerkraut Relish on Hoagie Rolls

4 sandwiches

When working on the farm all day, it was easy to start the charcoal grill during morning chores and toss a bunch of fruit and veggies on to slow cook. Onions, eggplant and apples were best suited to this leave-it-alone method and I have included at least one recipe for each in this book. Here is one way to use those sweet, soft, caramelized and smoky onions. If you do not have a grill or time for grilling, it is easy enough to set the onions in the oven to roast (see below).

4 hoagie rolls

4 bratwurst (and or tofu bratwurst)

4 tbsp stone ground mustard

2 tbsp mayonnaise

1 medium Walla Walla sweet onion

1 ½ c sauerkraut well drained

½ tbsp fresh cracked pepper

½ tsp table salt

1 tbsp olive oil

If you do not have a grill or time to grill the onions, you can cook them in the oven as noted here. Pre-heat the oven to 450 degrees. Set the top oven rack about 8" below the broiler. Cut the onion into 8ths and place in a mixing bowl. Add the salt and olive oil. Stir until coated. Place on a sheet pan and spread out evenly. Set on the top rack of the oven. Check after 10 minutes. When the onions have softened and started to brown, turn on the broiler. Keep a careful eye on the onions when the broiler is on. You should pull the onions from the oven when they are starting to brown all over but before they burn. Some onions will be more browned than others. Set aside to cool. Turn off the oven.

Slice open the Hoagie rolls and toast briefly in the still warm oven.

Boil the bratwursts according to package directions.

Chop the cooled onions and add to a small mixing bowl along with the sauerkraut, pepper, salt and mayonnaise.

Build your sandwich by spreading mustard on one side of each toasted hoagie roll. A ½ c of the onion mixture on the other side of the hoagie roll and tuck the bratwurst down the middle. Serve immediately.

Three Cheese with Chips on Whole Wheat Toast

1 sandwich

During my college years in Bellingham, I would take a Greyhound bus to Seattle on occasion to stay with friends at the University of Washington. On lower Capitol Hill, near one friend's walk-up apartment, there was a corner grocery store which made a super sandwich for about three dollars. I would buy one and a bag of cheese flavored tortilla chips to take back to the apartment for lunch or dinner. Once there, I would add ½ a bag of chips, a little salt onto the avocado and all of the black pepper from two of those little black and white paper pepper packets (where you rip off one side and pour the pepper out of the two little raised paper ridges). It always tasted perfect and here is how I make this sandwich at home.

2 slices wheat bread

2 tbsp cream cheese

½ avocado

3 large slices beefsteak tomato (such as Kellogg's Breakfast, Brandywine, Cherokee Purple)

1 slice provolone

1 sm bag of your favorite potato chips

1 tbsp mayonnaise

2 leaves Black Seeded Simpson lettuce (or other tender green leaf)

1 slice cheddar

1 large dill pickle sliced long and thin

1 tbsp Dijon mustard

pinch of salt

fresh cracked pepper

Lightly toast the bread. Spread the cream cheese over one slice of bread. Sprinkle with pepper. Gently mash the avocado onto the cream cheese. Sprinkle with salt. Cover with the tomato slices. Sprinkle the tomato slices with pepper. Add the provolone. Carefully arrange a handful of chips over the provolone. Spread the mayonnaise onto the lettuce and put it face down over the chips. Add the slice of cheddar. Add the slices of pickle. Spread the mustard on the last piece of bread and cover the pickles. Smash the sandwich together with the palm of your hand (just like my dad does to all of his sandwiches) and then slice in half and enjoy.

Wilted Spinach Croissant

4 sandwiches

At sixteen, I took a job in a small family-owned restaurant. The family was Persian, the food was Italian, and I was a dishwasher, barista, prep cook and server. When I was lucky, the sister/sister-in-law team in the back would share the Persian food they cooked on the side (I never imagined that rice/lima beans and dill could taste so good!!). On the other hand, all the Italian dishes they made were delicious and this sandwich, in my best estimation, was made up as something to do with leftover pasta sauce ingredients. It was so good that it became a staple on the lunch menu. Here is my version.

4 croissants

1 small yellow onion diced fine

2 tbsp olive oil

8 c packed chiffonade of spinach

2 tbsp mayonnaise

1 tsp kosher salt

½ tsp fresh cracked pepper

pinch of freshly grated nutmeg

1 tsp lemon juice

4 slices Swiss cheese

Finely dice the onions. Heat the olive oil in a small skillet and add the onions. Sauté the onions until soft but do not brown. Wash the spinach and then chiffonade the spinach while still damp. When the onions are soft, add the damp spinach to the skillet and place a lid on the skillet. Allow the spinach to wilt for several minutes. When the spinach has wilted, remove the lid and allow the liquid to evaporate. Add the mayonnaise, salt, pepper, nutmeg and lemon juice. Stir to incorporate and check for seasoning. Slice the croissants in half lengthwise but leave the top and bottom attached. Set them on a baking sheet. Cover the bottom of each croissant with a substantial amount of spinach filling. Place a slice of Swiss cheese on the other half of each croissant. Broil until the cheese is bubbly and starting to brown. Close the sandwich and serve hot.

Tofu Sliders with Wasabi Mayonnaise

8 Sliders

These yummy little sandwiches are packed with flavor and just the ticket for a fun lunch, or as a more substantial appetizer at a casual party. Seasoned tofu, baked in a savory broth in the oven creates a sturdy and delicious filling. After years of making sandwiches with baked tofu, I do think this slider with the wasabi mayonnaise and pickled ginger is my favorite!

8 whole wheat dinner rolls

1 pkg firm tofu (you cannot substitute silken tofu)

<u>Marinade</u>

¼ c soy sauce

2 tbsp water

¼ tsp cumin powder

¼ tsp granulated garlic

¼ tsp black pepper

pinch red pepper flakes

4 leaves Black Seeded Simpson lettuce (or other tender green leaf)

8 thick slices of tomato (such as Kellogg's Breakfast or Muskvich)

¼ c mayonnaise

1 tbsp wasabi paste

¼ c pickled ginger

Move the oven rack to the middle and preheat the oven to 400 degrees. Cut the tofu into 8 rectangle slices. Lay the pieces flat in the bottom of an 8x8" baking dish. Mix the soy sauce and water together and pour over the tofu. In a small dish, mix the cumin, garlic, pepper and pepper flakes. Sprinkle evenly over the tofu. Place in the oven on the middle shelf and bake for 25-30 minutes. Much of the sauce should evaporate and the tops of the tofu slices should begin to dry out. Remove the tofu from the oven and turn the oven down to 250 degrees.

Slice open each dinner roll and lay flat on a baking sheet. Place into the oven to warm and gently toast while you prepare the rest of the sandwich fillings.

Wash the lettuce leaves, break into 8 equal pieces and set aside. Slice the tomato(s) into 8 thick sandwich slices. Drain the ginger and set aside. Mix the mayonnaise and wasabi paste together in a small bowl.

Remove the dinner rolls from the oven. To build your tofu sliders put 2 tsp of wasabi mayonnaise on one side of each dinner roll. Add a piece of lettuce and a fat slice of tomato over the wasabi mayonnaise. Slice each rectangle of tofu in half and stack these slices off center on the opposite side of each dinner roll. Add a few pieces of pickled ginger over the tofu. Serve.

SIDES

Polenta with Variations

Home Fries

Risotto with Mushrooms and Vermouth

Cornbread with Cheddar and Jalapenos

French Lentil with Spring Herbs

Sweet Potato Mash with Coconut and Lime

Cabbage Pancakes

Hearty Spring Greens Seven Ways

Sautéed French Breakfast Radishes with Steamed Spinach

Green Beans with Salt and Oil

Polenta with Variations

6 servings

I started to eat polenta as a meal during college. It was inexpensive and tasted good with Cajun seasoned red beans (also inexpensive). I ate polenta for the first time as a side dish at Kenai Backcountry Lodge on Skilak Lake in the late 90's. It was speckled with fresh herbs which had been lightly sautéed in butter and folded into the cooked polenta with goat cheese. It was delicious. Much better than the polenta I had made during college. Since that time, I have made numerous variations and tried many a "vegetarian alternative" constructed of polenta at various restaurants. It is one of my favorite side dishes.

4 c water

1 c polenta

¼ tsp salt

¾ c parmesan reggiano

2 tbsp butter

2 tbsp sage leaves

Bring the water to a boil in a large heavy bottomed pot. Add the salt. Slowly pour in the polenta while stirring constantly. Turn down the heat to low and allow the polenta to simmer and cook for about 30 minutes. Stir often with a flat bottom spoon. When the polenta has softened and thickened, turn off the heat. Add the grated parmesan cheese. Stir well to incorporate fully. Melt and brown the butter in a cast iron skillet. Once the butter has browned remove the skillet from the heat and add the sage leaves. Stir them carefully as they sizzle and become crisp. Pour the butter and sage leaves over the polenta in a serving dish or on individual plates.

Variations (For each variation, skip the addition of the butter and sage leaves):

Cool the polenta in a shallow dish. Slice into individual servings. Place in an oven proof dish. Cover with simmered red sauce (pg. 129) or pesto. Sprinkle with grated mozzarella. Broil until the cheese is melted and bubbly. Serve immediately.

Sauté mushrooms in butter and vermouth. Top each serving.

Sauté some sweet red peppers and Walla Walla sweet onions in olive oil with a pinch of salt, a pinch of sugar and dash of balsamic vinegar for seasoning. Top each serving.

Home Fries

4 servings

Home fries are not just for breakfast! Potatoes are such a delicious side dish and home fries are excellent not only when served for breakfast with eggs and sausage, but also for dinner alongside a nice roasted chicken, or even tucked inside a tortilla with beans and cheese for a hearty lunch. I always like to use a little bit of onion when I make home fries and toss in a piece of green pepper when I have it on hand. Add a pinch of paprika at the end of cooking to give them their lovely red color.

    1 small Rossa di Milano onion diced

    ½ green pepper diced

    2 c cubed russet potato (about 2 medium potatoes)

    4 tbsp olive oil

    1 tsp paprika

    kosher salt

    fresh cracked pepper

Heat 1 tbsp olive oil in a cast iron skillet. Add the diced onion and green pepper. Sauté until they are soft and starting to brown. Remove the green pepper and onions from the skillet to a small bowl and set aside. Peel and dice the potatoes into ½" x ½" cubes. Heat a cast iron skillet to medium heat and add 3 tbsp of olive oil and all of the potatoes, toss to coat. Cook the potatoes slowly, allowing them to brown completely on one side before flipping them over, and letting them brown again. When potatoes have browned on most sides and are soft throughout (about 15 minutes) add the paprika. Toss and stir the potatoes a few more minutes to coat with the paprika and allow the flavor to bloom in the heat and oil. Turn off the heat and add the cooked onions and peppers. Season the potatoes to taste with kosher salt and fresh cracked pepper. Serve warm.

Risotto with Mushrooms and Vermouth

6 servings

Risotto is such a nice and exotic sounding name for a rice dish. In order to make risotto properly you do need to have a short grained Italian rice on hand. Either Arborio or carnaroli rice yield the proper creamy texture to a finished batch of risotto. Arborio is much more common and easier to find in a regular grocery store. Far less common but available in gourmet shops, carnaroli is a traditional risotto variety from Italy. For years, I only ordered risotto, or entrees which came with risotto, at restaurants. This is because I did not think I could make risotto on my own. However, it is actually not that difficult to make at home. You just need to be able to cut up a few vegetables and stir. The one tricky part about risotto is the recommendation to stir almost constantly. This is something you do not necessarily need to do at home. Instead, you can stir heartily just after you add each addition of stock and then let the risotto rest while the liquid is absorbed and repeat. Risotto is exquisite. Good luck and have fun!

1 flat bottomed wooded spoon or spatula

½ lb crimini mushrooms

¼ Walla Walla sweet onion

1 tbsp olive oil

1 tsp lemon juice

1 ½ c arborio rice (or carnaroli)

½ c dry vermouth (or substitute white wine)

4 c mushroom stock (4 c water, 2 tbsp porcini powder, 1 tsp salt OR substitute vegetable or chicken stock)

1 tbsp butter

4 tbsp parmesan reggiano

kosher salt

fresh cracked black pepper

Slice and sauté the mushrooms and onions in olive oil in a large cooking pot over medium heat until soft and tender but not limp. Remove from the heat to a small bowl and toss with the lemon juice. In a second cooking pot, bring the mushroom stock to a boil and turn off the heat (you can do this while sautéing the mushrooms and onions). Add the rice to the same cooking pot in which you cooked the mushrooms and onions. On medium heat, pour in the vermouth and stir with the flat bottomed wooden spoon until the vermouth has been absorbed by the rice. Add one cup of the stock to the pot and stir the rice slowly until the liquid has been reduced by half. When the second half of the liquid has been absorbed, add ½ cup of the hot stock and stir gently. Use a flat bottomed spoon to scrape the bottom clear of any rice or cooked-on caramelized bits. Let the rice rest and absorb the rest of the stock. Adjust the heat down if the rice is sticking quite a bit to the bottom of the pot. Continue to add the stock in ½ c increments until all the stock has been added and absorbed. Turn the heat down to low. Taste the rice for texture. It should be "al dente", just the soft side of crunchy. If your rice is still crunchy in the middle, add hot water in ½ cup additions until the rice is al dente. When the rice is ready, add the butter and stir vigorously until it is melted and incorporated. Add the mushroom and onion mixture and the parmesan. Stir until the cheese has melted. Taste and adjust the seasoning with salt and pepper. Serve warm.

Cornbread with Cheddar and Jalapenos

9 servings

There are as many variations to cornbread as there are palettes. You may prefer your corn bread sweet and slathered in butter and honey, or unsweetened at the bottom of a bowl of chili, or crisp from a cast iron skillet to round out a home cooked chicken dinner. Personally, my favorite is packed with chilies, cheese and green onions right out of the cast iron skillet.

1 c cornmeal

1c flour

1 tbsp sugar

1 tbsp baking powder

½ tsp table salt

1 c milk

1/3 c olive oil

1 egg

½ c shredded medium cheddar cheese

1 small can roasted green chilies (hot or mild your choice)

4 Evergreen Hardy White scallions chopped fine

2 tsp shortening

Preheat the oven to 400 degrees. Put the shortening into a medium cast iron skillet and put into the oven to melt. Whisk the dry ingredients together in one bowl. Measure the milk and olive oil into another bowl, add the egg and whisk them all together. Make a well in the center of the dry ingredients, pour in the wet and gently stir them all together. Fold in the cheese, roasted chilies and green onions. Carefully remove the cast iron skillet from the oven and swirl the melted shortening around the edges. Pour the batter into the skillet and return it to the oven. Bake in the oven for about 22 minutes until a toothpick inserted in the center comes out clean. Cool at least 10 minutes before slicing.

French Lentils with Spring Herbs

Makes approximately 4 cups

For years and years, I had no idea there was more than one kind of lentil! What a surprise for me, and much to the chagrin of Jeff to whom a lentil is a lentil is a lentil and he would rather not eat them. In the spring on the farm, the herbs were always bountiful and rebounding quickly from their winter hibernation. This recipe came about in particular when we were thinning the basil plantings. A tiny basil seedling is delicious tossed into a lentil salad with lots of other herbs. The only way I know of to get ahold of baby basil seedlings to eat, is to grow them yourself. Yet the salad is still wonderful without the basil.

1 c dry French lentils

3 c vegetable stock (or water)

2 tbsp EVOO

½ tsp salt (adjust according to taste if you use stock or water)

½ tsp finely ground black pepper

½ lemon juiced

½ a lemon zested

1 c minced Italian parsley

2 tbsp chopped fresh herbs (chives, rosemary, oregano, sage, thyme, lemon balm)

1 handful basil sprouts (optional)

Bring the lentils to boil in a pot with the stock or water. Cook until soft. Drain well and cool. When completely cool add the olive oil, lemon juice and zest, minced parsley and chopped herbs. Mix well. Season with salt to taste.

Sweet Potato Mash with Coconut Milk and Lime

4 servings

Jeff and I spent some time in Australia a few years ago on our way home from Antarctica. While there, we joined a couple at their farm place in the country. Walking around their farm, you could see kangaroos at dusk. And although we looked and looked, we never spotted a koala, which were also in the area. One night for dinner, they threw this sweet potato mash together as a side dish. Back home in Alaska, a friend makes an awesome sweet potato dish with garlic and lime. This flavor combination here is just as spectacular!

  2 large sweet potatoes

  ½ lime juiced

  ½ lime zested

  6 tbsp coconut milk

Peel and cut the sweet potatoes into large chunks. Set them in a pot and cover them with water. Bring to a boil on the stove until the sweet potatoes are soft. Drain them in a colander and put them in a large mixing bowl. Add the lime juice, zest and coconut milk. Mash this all together until smooth. Serve hot.

Cabbage Pancakes

8 – 3" pancakes

In Japan, there are many, many variations of a cabbage pancake. Some have corn, others shrimp, and others are cooked on top of a pile of noodles. There are even restaurants which specialize in making these pancakes. Sometimes you order all the ingredients you want and cook them on a griddle in the middle of the table. Other times you sit at a long bar in front of a griddle, and the cook makes yours to order right in front of you. I was suspicious the first time I ate one of these that it would be any good at all, or filling for that matter. Maybe I love cabbage more that I realize, but these are actually really yummy. Here is a very basic and easy to make at home cabbage pancake. Sometimes I cook and serve only these for dinner. Sometimes I serve them as a side dish.

    4 c Des Vertus savoy cabbage (or substitute Napa cabbage or another green savoy cabbage)

    2 medium Danvers carrots (or substitute any carrot)

    4 Evergreen Hardy White Scallions (or substitute green onions)

    ¾ c flour

    2 tbsp corn starch

    1 egg

    ½ tsp kosher salt

    ½ tsp finely ground black pepper

    ¾ c water

    1 tbsp olive oil

    mayonnaise

    hot sauce (siracha or chili oil)

1 sheet of nori (sushi roll wrapper)

Shred the cabbage and grate the carrots into a very large mixing bowl. Chop the green onions and add them to the bowl. Sprinkle the flour, corn starch, salt and pepper over the vegetables and then mix them well to coat. Crack the eggs into the bowl and add the water. Stir everything together. You should have a batter the thickness of thin yogurt coating all of the vegetables. Heat up some olive oil to medium heat on a griddle or in a cast iron skillet. Spoon the batter and vegetables out onto the hot surface and squash the pancake flat with the back of your spatula. These are best when cooked slowly so keep an eye on the temperature. Put a lid on the pan and cook for 3 minutes. Remove the lid and cook uncovered for 3 more minutes after flipping. Serve in a pile on a plate spread with mayonnaise, a dash of hot sauce and crushed up nori (just smash up one sushi wrapper with your fingers into green confetti and sprinkle over the pancakes).

Hearty Spring Greens Seven Ways

2 servings

Spring greens are tender and can be steamed quickly in a sauce pan with a lid. Once wilted spring greens can be finished in a number of ways to match your entrée or taste buds. When I was little, my parents had a few acres of property on the edge of town. Several families from church kept gardens on the big side lot. One Dad in particular would rope you into helping him out with his garden more often than I ever thought I wanted to help out. To boot, whenever they stayed over for potluck dinner, this Dad would bring kale into the house to feed us. Yuck-o-rama is all I could ever think about kale. My distinct memory of cooked kale is that it was grey and stinky. That is a distant memory. Now as an adult, I have learned to not ever cook kale for more than about 8 minutes. I have also learned to select the finest, youngest leaves to eat. And so I do actually like kale. You and your family, as it turns out, may also be fans.

8 oz hearty spring greens (kale, chard, beet tops, mustard greens etc.)

2 tbsp olive oil

Wash greens and leave damp. Toss them into a sauce pan over medium heat with the olive oil. Stir gently then place the lid onto the sauce pan. Allow to steam for 4-5 minutes until completely wilted (chard and beet greens will cook faster than mustard and kale greens). Finish the greens by adding one of the options below and gently turning over until incorporated and warmed throughout. Serve immediately.

1. Add fresh cracked black pepper. Stir to incorporate. Plate up and sprinkle with a finishing salt (lemon, truffle, smoked, sea).

2. Add 2 tbsp white wine or dry vermouth, fresh cracked pepper and salt.

3. Add 1 tbsp lemon juice, fresh cracked pepper and salt.

4. Add 2 tbsp mayonnaise and fresh cracked pepper.

5. Add 1 tbsp soy sauce and 1 tbsp sesame oil. Plate up and sprinkle with roasted sesame seeds

6. Add 2 tbsp of your favorite salad dressing.

7. Add 1 tbsp of tahini and 1 tbsp of soy sauce.

Sautéed French Breakfast Radish with Steamed Spinach

4 servings

Of all the radishes out there and there are a lot more that I thought, the French breakfast radish is my personal favorite. They are crisp, sweet and spicy all balanced perfectly. The slender cylinder of growth, and red color fading to rose to white is beautiful on any plate or in any dish. The thing about radishes I did not know until just about four years ago, is that they are really, really good sautéed in butter. I mean really good. I could not sauté up enough of them the first time I tried this at home. And I am not above leaving out the steamed spinach of this recipe altogether. However, it is a very nice combination and it looks awesome when you plate it up.

1 bunch French breakfast radishes

1 bunch spinach

1 – 2 tbsp butter

kosher salt

fresh cracked pepper

Steam the spinach and arrange on platter in a nest. Thinly slice the radishes into disks. Heat 1 ½ tbsp butter in a pan until foaming subsides. Add radishes and sauté quickly until just browning on both sides. Turn out into the spinach nest. Finish with salt and freshly ground pepper. Eat immediately.

Green Beans with Salt and Oil

4 servings

I have eaten green beans, often from a can for my whole life. Most certainly, green bean casserole had been the pinnacle of green bean dishes until I had a chance to spend a weekend at a remote fly in lodge on the Alaskan Peninsula. It was here for the first time I ate fresh boiled green beans dressed only with VERY good olive oil and kosher salt. I was suspicious that the adage "food eaten while in remote areas where food is not expected to be amazingly delicious is no longer delicious when you make it at home" perhaps would hold true. I made these at home. Yum. Naturally, on the farm, we had green beans in such abundance that they would weigh down the bean poles, and pull them all to the ground overnight. We ate beans like this a lot.

4 handfuls fresh Kentucky Wonder Pole beans

EVOO of top quality and flavor

kosher salt (or lemon salt, or black salt, or red Hawaiian salt, or cypress smoked salt…)

Bring a pot of water with a steamer insert to boil. Pinch the ends off of and pull the strings out of your beans. After all that work I rarely bother to cut up the beans, leaving that instead to whoever will be eating them when they are finished. Add the green beans to the steamer basket and cook them until tender but still bright green. Remove the beans from the steamer and place on a serving dish. Drizzle with EVOO and sprinkle with a salt of your choice.

PASTA & PIZZA

Orecchiette with Parsley and Garlic

Angel Hair with Swiss Chard and Peanuts

Tuscan Kale Carbonara

Fava Beans and Chive Blossom Bulgur

Simmered Red Sauce from Canned Tomato

Blue Cheese & Walnut Garden Fresh Linguini

Israeli Couscous with Sun-dried Tomatoes and Fresh Peas

Spicy Cold Soba Salad

Mushroom Pizza

Caramelized Onion and Smoked Blue Cheese Pizza

Spinach & Three Cheese Calzone

Orecchiette with Parsley and Garlic

4 servings

My exposure to pasta as I was growing up included spaghetti feed fund raisers, macaroni salads at summer barbecue's, and butter and parmesan egg noodle side dishes on the family dinner table. As an adult it has been fun to explore new pasta shapes by ordering a dish at a restaurant or finding something interesting in the aisle of a gourmet grocery store. The shape of pasta goes a long way in affecting the taste of the finished product. My nieces and nephews are convinced that spiral macaroni and cheese is much better than elbow macaroni and cheese, and I think I have to agree with them. Orecchiette pasta looks like tiny hats, although the name means tiny ears. It is just perfect for catching little bits of garlic and parsley, so every bite is both simple and satisfying.

1 lb dried orecchiette

½ c fresh Italian parsley

8 cloves heirloom garlic such as Polish Softneck

4 tbsp butter

3 tbsp olive oil

2 tbsp pasta cooking water

kosher salt

fresh ground pepper

2 tbsp parmesan reggiano

Cook the pasta al dente according to package instructions. Finely chop the Italian Parsley and the garlic. Melt the butter in a sauté pan and then add the olive oil. When the butter and olive oil are hot, add the garlic and sauté until soft. Add the parsley and stir until just wilted. Drain the pasta. Add the pasta and reserved pasta water to the sauté pan with garlic and parsley. Toss to coat. Add salt and pepper to taste. Plate and then freshly grate some parmesan reggiano over the top of the pasta. Enjoy!

Angel Hair with Swiss Chard and Peanuts

4 servings

This pasta dish is quick and easy to make and reminiscent of pad thai. I have spent hours in the kitchen trying to perfect homemade pad thai. I have made countless trips to the bathroom at various Thai restaurants only to detour past the open door to the kitchen or back pantry and take a peek at which brand of fish sauce and curry pastes they are using. One little Thai restaurant I used to drop by a couple of times a summer was a kick, because the owner/server/greeter was usually asleep on the floor behind the cash register when you came in the front door. He would jump up when the little bells on the door jingled, grab a couple of menus and show you to a seat. The pad thai here was always better than any I have recreated at home. However, this pasta with Swiss chard and peanuts makes me remember the taste of pad thai without feeling like I have turned out a dish that is not quite right. If you would like to do so, you can easily add grilled tofu or shrimp to this pasta.

8 oz angel hair pasta

8 oz Red Rhubarb chard (or other Swiss chard)

3 cloves heirloom garlic such as Polish Softneck

1 tbsp olive oil

pinch salt

3 tbsp soy sauce

2 tbsp dark roasted sesame oil

1 tsp brown sugar

pinch dried red chili flakes

¼ c crushed peanuts

4 each Evergreen Hardy White scallions

1 tbsp lime juice

1 tbsp toasted sesame seeds (optional)

Wash the Swiss chard and separate the ribs from the leaves. Separately chop the leaves and ribs into bite-sized pieces. Peel and finely chop the garlic cloves. In a medium sauté pan, heat the oil on medium high and add the garlic and a pinch of salt. Stir continuously until the garlic is soft but not brown. Add the chopped Swiss chard leaves and 2 tablespoons of water. Continue to stir until the chard has completely wilted. Turn off the heat and set aside. Cook the pasta according to the package directions. Add the Swiss chard ribs along with the pasta to the boiling water. When the pasta is al dente, drain it in a colander and return it to the warm cooking pot. Add the soy sauce and toss the pasta until it has completely absorbed the soy sauce. Add the sesame oil and toss to coat. Add the sautéed Swiss chard and garlic, tossing the pasta to mix. Add the sugar, dried red chili flakes, crushed peanuts and chopped spring onions reserving some peanuts and spring green onions to use as a garnish. Toss the pasta to mix. Turn out the pasta into a serving dish or platter. Sprinkle with the lime juice and garnish with the reserved spring green onions and peanuts. Sprinkle all over with the toasted sesame seeds.

Tuscan Kale Carbonara

4 servings

For sure, every time we were selling kale at the farmers market, someone would mention just how delicious kale was when cooked with bacon. Now, to be clear, isn't everything a little better when cooked with bacon? Anyway, it got me thinking about bacon dishes and this led to carbonara, which was one of the main pasta dishes served at a little Italian café that I worked at in high school. What if we swapped the peas that the Persian lady at the café always tossed in with her carbonara, with good ole Tuscan kale? Try it for yourself, easy and oh so delicious.

8 oz spaghetti

4 oz Tuscan kale (Dinosaur, Nero di Toscana, Lacinato)

4 thick slices peppered bacon

3 eggs

¾ c finely grated parmesan reggiano

½ lemon juice

kosher salt (need depending upon how salty your bacon happens to be)

fresh cracked pepper

Cook the spaghetti al dente according to package directions. Tear the kale from the stems and give it a rinse in the sink. Cook the bacon in a large skillet (which has a lid to use later). Set the bacon aside and drain the grease from the skillet but do not wipe it out. Add the damp kale to the pan on low heat. Put on the lid until it has wilted. Stir once or twice to mix in the bacon grease. In a small mixing bowl whip the eggs. Grate the parmesan and set it aside. When the pasta has finished cooking, toss it while still very hot into a large skillet (no heat) and add the eggs and 2/3 of the parmesan cheese. Toss this combination for a couple of minutes to "cook" the eggs. Add the bacon, kale, lemon juice and remaining cheese. Toss again. Taste for salt and adjust as necessary. If you would like your sauce more cooked, turn on the heat under the skillet to high and keep the pasta moving around. When the pan has come up to heat, turn the heat off immediately. Serve with fresh cracked pepper.

Fava Bean and Chive Blossom Bulgur

4 servings

The first time I cooked fava beans was the second winter I was married. In a little gourmet shop, I had picked up a pretty package of dried fava beans that also had a recipe on the back. One night, clever me, I decided to make not one, but three different dried bean dishes for dinner. Thinking of course that if, instead of eating at home, we had popped into some very groovy café, a dinner option might be three little bean salads from behind the glass case with a nice glass of red wine. Well, my dear sweet husband, never one to proclaim he likes eating beans of any kind was, needless to say, very polite that night. I have never repeated that "dinner". Fast forward to the farm where we grew fava beans as a winter cover crop on the fields. Whoa nelly! Fresh fava beans are a whole different story and worth every single bit of effort to boil and remove from the pod and then peel. This combination of fava beans with chive blossoms makes a very tasty and very pretty dish. I hope that you not only can get your hands on fresh fava beans and chive blossoms someday but that you really like this combination.

    1 c bulgur

    1 c fresh fava beans (boiled and peeled)*

    2 cloves heirloom garlic such as Polish Softneck

    2 small shallots

    1 tbsp olive oil

    ½ tsp kosher salt

    2 tsp lemon juice

    2 tbsp EVOO

    3 chive flowers

    ½ c crumbled Feta

Bring two cups of water to a boil and add the bulgur. Return to a boil and then turn off the heat and cover with a lid for ten minutes. If you have not done so already, remove the fava beans from the pods, and blanch them in boiling water for just a minute. Drain and cool them immediately in an ice water bath. Peel the fava beans a second time revealing the bright green yummy interior bean. This is what you will add to the bulgur. Chop the garlic and shallots and sauté them up until tender in the olive oil and ½ tsp kosher salt. When they are soft, add the fava beans and toss gently until warm. Add this to the pot with the bulgur (check the bulgur first that it is tender). Add the lemon juice to the sauté pan and warm gently scraping any bits loose off the bottom of the pan. Add this to the bulgur along with the EVOO and toss well to mix. Remove the small purple chive blossoms from the big chive flowers. Reserve a teaspoon of blossoms and toss the rest in with the bulgur and fava beans. Put the bulgur onto a serving plate and sprinkle with crumbled feta and the remaining chive blossoms.

*1 lb unpeeled fava beans in pods = approximately 1 cup of peeled beans

Simmered Red Sauce from Canned Tomato

4 - 6 servings

When I say "canned tomato", what I mean in an ideal world are home canned tomatoes. Home canned tomatoes made from wonderful Amish paste, Opalka paste or San Marzano tomatoes. Although to be honest, more often than not on the farm, the tomatoes which ended up in canning jars were the ones so ugly that no one would buy them or so bountiful we could just not sell them all. So, my canning jars of tomatoes were a smorgasbord of Kellogg's Breakfast, Cherokee Purple, Moskvich, Brandywine and paste tomatoes all tasting just like sunshine. Next to home canned tomatoes, and currently my option, are whole peeled canned tomatoes. I made this sauce many times on the farm. It is simple and delicious. I love it over ravioli with fresh shaved parmesan or more simply with spaghetti and a dollop of fresh ricotta.

1 28 oz can of whole peeled tomatoes (or 1 quart jar of home canned tomatoes)

4 cloves Chesnok Red garlic (or other garlic)

½ tsp salt

1 tbsp fresh Italian parsley

1 tsp fresh rosemary

2 Tbsp EVOO

1 tsp balsamic vinegar

pinch of crushed red chilies

pinch of sugar

Add the tomatoes to a sauce pan on the stove which has a lid. Peel and chop the garlic and add this to the pan. Roughly snip one tablespoon of parsley and add it to the pan. Add the rest of the ingredients and simmer covered for 20 minutes. Remove the lid and continue to simmer until reduced by one third. Stir occasionally and break up the large pieces of tomato with a spoon. Taste and adjust the seasoning. Serve as recommended above.

Blue Cheese & Walnut Garden Fresh Linguini

4 servings

A stop in the garden to collect some fresh tasty bits for dinner is one of life's simple pleasures. Jeff grew up in California and they always had a lemon tree in a pot out on the deck. When we moved to the farm, we kept a Meyer lemon tree in one corner of a hoop house. And so, we could pop into the hoop house after work, grab a handful of cherry tomatoes, a bunch of fresh Italian parsley and one Meyer lemon to take into the house and make this yummy pasta dish.

8 oz linguini

¼ c toasted walnuts

1 medium shallot (about 3 tbsp chopped)

1 tbsp olive oil

1 c chopped Italian parsley

1 pint Red Pear mini tomatoes

½ c half & half

¼ c pasta water

4 oz blue cheese

juice of 1 small Meyer Lemon

kosher salt

fresh cracked black pepper

Bring a pot of water to boil for the pasta and cook the linguini according to package directions. While the pasta is cooking prepare the sauce. Carefully toast ¼ c of walnuts in a skillet and then run through a nut mill to chop them up. Chop the shallot finely and sauté until soft in 1 tablespoon of olive oil and ½ teaspoon salt over medium heat. Finely chop the parsley and halve the cherry tomatoes, and add into the sauté pan with the shallots. Stir until the parsley has wilted. Add the half & half, ¼ cup of the pasta water, 3 tablespoons of chopped walnuts and 3 ounces of crumbled blue cheese. Stir and allow the cheese to incorporate into the sauce. Do not let the sauce boil. Squeeze in the juice of ½ the lemon. Drain the cooked pasta and add the pasta to the sauce. Toss until coated, turn off the heat and let the pasta rest for about 2 minutes. Serve garnished with the reserved blue cheese and walnuts.

Israeli Couscous with Sun-dried Tomatoes and Fresh Peas

4 servings

Sun-dried tomatoes are one of those foods which seem like a delicacy to me. I am sure the first time I ate them was chopped up in cream cheese at a bagel shop I loved in Bellingham during college. For a while, every chance I had to eat a bagel anywhere, I would order one with sun-dried tomato something or another. On the farm, we decided to grow the Principe Borghese cherry tomato. It was like a little paste tomato and perfect for drying. And we did so by the small bushel. They were so very delicious and just the thing to have tucked away in the cupboard for the winter. This recipe uses early peas from the hoop houses and lots of sun dried tomatoes from the pantry.

- 2 c Israeli pearl couscous
- ½ c sun dried Principe Borghese cherry tomatoes (or other sun-dried tomato)
- 2 tbsp shallots
- 1 tbsp olive oil
- ¾ c fresh peas
- 1 tsp kosher salt
- ¼ tsp fresh cracked pepper

Bring 3 cups of water to a boil. Pour ½ cup of water over the sun dried tomatoes in a bowl to re-hydrate them. Add the couscous to the rest of the water and bring it back to a boil. Cover and reduce to a simmer and cook for 10 minutes. Finely chop the shallots. In a large skillet, sauté the shallots in olive oil until they are soft and translucent. Chop up the softened sun-dried tomatoes and add them along with the peas to the skillet. Toss until warm through. Add the vegetables, salt and pepper to the cooked couscous. Mix well and taste for seasoning. If dry, add a few tablespoons of the soaking water from the sun dried tomatoes. This dish is good served hot or as a cold salad.

Spicy Cold Soba Salad

6 servings

I remember eating buckwheat pancakes when I was a child and thinking they were super delicious. As an adult, living and working in Japan, I fell in love with soba noodles. And it was in Japan that I learned buckwheat and soba are the same grain. So perhaps my taste memory sprang forward when I had my first bit of soba noodles? This spicy salad combines the hearty soba noodle with fresh chopped Swiss chard and a spicy creamy dressing with a citrus twist. A perfect make-ahead-salad that you can pack for your lunch.

4 skeins soba noodles

2 tbsp soy sauce

1 tbsp lemon juice

3 tbsp mayonnaise

2 tsp siracha

½ tsp kosher salt

¼ tsp fresh ground black pepper

8 oz Red Rhubarb chard (or other Swiss chard or spinach) chopped

1 tbsp olive oil

1 bunch Evergreen Hardy White scallions chopped

2 tbsp sesame seeds (toasted)

Cook noodles according to package directions. Drain and rinse until cool in cold water. Mix the soy sauce, lemon juice, mayonnaise, siracha, kosher salt and fresh ground black pepper together in a small bowl. Strip the Swiss chard leaves from the ribs and cut or tear into bite-sized pieces and set aside. Chop the ribs into small chunks. In a sauté pan heat 1 tablespoon of olive oil until it shimmers and then add the Swiss chard ribs. Sauté the Swiss chard ribs until soft then add the leaves, turn down the heat and cover the pan until the leaves have wilted. Once wilted, remove from heat and cool under cold running water. Toss the noodles, Swiss chard, dressing, chopped green onions (reserve some for garnish) and sesame seeds together in a large bowl until well coated. Garnish with a few slivers of green onion and some toasted sesame seeds.

Mushroom Pizza

1 - 12" pizza

A note on pizza:

This is perhaps my favorite dish. I have few pizza boundaries. It is my weakness and I am not ashamed. If there is an option of pizza, I will take it. That option may be a frozen hockey puck of pizza from an Alaskan State Ferry galley, a greasy old slice from the heated slab at the grocery store, the hot slice for a buck ninety nine at everyone's favorite warehouse shopping store, the pizza ordered for a party by someone else and covered with toppings I do not even like (I pull them off and set them aside, eating whatever remains), a cowboy/cowgirl pizza as we call it that you can order from a chain shop on the corner that makes-em how you like-em to take home and bake in your own oven or this fine homemade example. I did not even mention the number of very fine locally owned pizza establishments I have visited in my lifetime. Yes, my favorite restaurant is anything that serves pizza.

A note on pizza dough:

You can buy a pre-made crust to use, build the pizza on English muffins like my mom used to do, use thick sturdy pita like I do in a hurry, use fresh dough purchased from a store in the refrigerator isle or from a local pizza parlor, buy frozen bread dough and use it as pizza crust or make your own. If you make your own, you can use the recipe below and have the dough ready to go in 1 hour or less if you are in a hurry. Or if you happen to be a fan of no-knead refrigerator doughs, you can use one of those. I prefer refrigerator fermented dough when I have planned ahead, but find the dough below perfectly satisfactory for a homemade pizza at the last minute.

Dough

makes 2 – 12" pizzas

2 ½ tsp dry active yeast

1 c warm water

2 ½ c all purpose flour

2 tbsp olive oil

1 tsp salt

Add the yeast and olive oil to the water and stir to incorporate. Add the flour and mix until it pulls away from the sides of the bowl and makes a ball. Let it rest for 5 minutes. Pull the dough out on to a working surface, flatten it and sprinkle with the salt. Knead for 5 minutes. Place the dough into a well oiled bowl and cover with a damp cloth or piece of plastic wrap. Set aside in a warm place until you are ready to use.

Using your hands, flatten a softball-sized piece of dough into a disk on a well floured surface. Stretch and flatten the dough with your fingers into an 8" round. Let the dough rest while you make the sauce. After resting, stretch and flatten the dough with your fingers into a 12 -14" disk, 1/8-1/4" thick. Be sure to keep the dough floured so it will not stick to the working surface. If you are using a pizza peel, add 1 tablespoon of corn meal under the dough once the full size has been achieved and check to be sure you can move the dough around the peel on top of the cornmeal. If you are using a baking pan lightly oil the pan before placing the flattened dough onto the pan. You can also use parchment paper under your dough and in that case, no need to lightly oil or cornmeal the surface.

Sauce

makes enough for 2 – 12" pizzas

14 oz can whole peeled tomatoes (or 1 pint jar of home canned tomatoes)

splash of balsamic vinegar

1 tsp kosher salt

1 tsp basil

1 tsp oregano

1 tsp granulated garlic

Place the tomatoes, salt and herbs into a bowl and blend completely into a uniform puree using an immersion blender. Set aside. Any unused sauce can be frozen for your next pizza.

Topping

makes enough for 1 – 12" pizza

1 c sliced crimini mushrooms

1 ½ c shredded mozzarella

1 tbsp EVOO

Build:

Cover the dough with sauce being sure to spread it all the way to the very edges. Spread one cup of mozzarella over the sauce. Evenly distribute the crimini mushrooms over the cheese. Finish with the remaining cheese and drizzle the whole pizza with the EVOO.

Bake:

Place your oven rack at the very top of the oven. If you have a pizza stone, place it on this top rack. Pre-heat the oven to 450 degrees. Bake the pizza on the top rack for 15-18 minutes. The dough on the bottom and the cheese on the top should both be browning. Remove from the oven and let rest for about 5 minutes before slicing and eating.

Caramelized Onion and Smoked Blue Cheese Pizza

1 - 12" pizza

I was in college when I first heard about using caramelized onions as 'sauce' for your pizza from the captain of the *Snow Goose*. What a flavor! Crumbling bits of blue cheese on top completes one of the best flavor combinations ever.

<u>Pizza Notes</u> (see page 136)

<u>Dough Recipe</u> (see page 136)

<u>Sauce</u>

makes enough for 1 - 12" pizza

1 large Walla Walla sweet onion sliced thin

2 tbsp EVOO

1 tsp kosher salt

2 tbsp brown sugar

Heat the oil in a fry pan with a lid large enough to accommodate the onion slices. When the oil starts to shimmer, add the onions and salt then cover with a lid. Allow to heat and wilt for about 5 minutes. Remove the lid and stir frequently until the onions have reduced in size and browned evenly, about 15 minutes. Add the brown sugar and stir frequently for about 5 more minutes. Turn off the heat and set aside until ready to use.

<u>Topping</u>

makes enough for 1 – 12" pizza

2 oz smoked blue cheese

½ tsp kosher salt

1 tbsp EVOO

Build:

Spread the onion sauce evenly over the prepared dough being sure to cover the dough all the way to the edges. Crumble the blue cheese over the top of the onions. Sprinkle with salt and drizzle with EVOO.

Bake:

Place your oven rack at the very top of the oven. If you have a pizza stone, place it on this top rack. Pre-heat the oven to 450 degrees. Bake the pizza on the top rack for 15-18 minutes. The dough on the bottom and the cheese on the top should both be browning. Remove from the oven and let rest for about 5 minutes before slicing and eating.

Spinach & Three Cheese Calzone

6 servings

The first calzone I ever remember eating was in a little, dark, run down restaurant building in Spokane near a college. I ordered a mushroom calzone and ever since, have tried my best to replicate the taste, look and flavor of that first calzone. Most impressive, and something I never have been able to pull off in my home oven, was the look of that first calzone. Like a Smurf cap. Tall, brown, thin and crisp and chewy and perfect as a calzone can be, in my mind. At this point, unless I get an indoor pizza oven or an outdoor wood-fired oven, I think I will just have to go back to Spokane every once and a while for one of these calzones. In the meantime here is a delicious spinach and three cheese version that I used to make while working in the kitchen at summer camp. Enjoy!

1 recipe dough (see pg 136)

1 recipe simmered red sauce (see pg 129)

4 oz shredded mozzarella

3 c baby spinach

2 oz grated parmesan reggiano

½ tsp kosher salt

4 oz cream cheese

Place your oven rack and pizza stone if you have one at the very top position in your oven. Pre-heat your oven to 425 degrees. Spread out the dough on a 13 x 9', oiled half sheet pan. Spread the sauce on one half leaving 1" around the edge to fold over later. Layer the mozzarella, spinach, and parmesan over the sauce. Sprinkle with a ½ tsp of salt. Cut the cream cheese into slices and dot across the top of the rest of the ingredients. Fold over the undecorated edge of dough and pinch and roll the edges together. Use a sharp knife and cut 4 - 6 slits in the dough across the top of the calzone. Place the calzones in a 425 degree oven on the top rack for 20 minutes. Check that the underside is done by gently lifting with a spatula to see that it has browned. Cool, slice, eat.

ENTRÉES

Roast Chicken

Bangers and Mash

Soy Ginger Salmon

Simple Salmon – Cyprus Smoked Salt & Lemon

Black Bean & Chicken Enchiladas with Roasted Poblano Sauce

Spring Curry from White Star Farms

Fish Cakes with Brown Rice and Lemon Sauce

Spring Rolls with Tofu and Peanut Sauce

Summer Squash Fritters (Super Easy or Fancy)

Poached Rockfish with Vegetable Relish

Skillet Cooked Peppered Tri-tip with Gremolata

Roast Chicken

1 whole chicken

The thing about roasting a chicken from the farm is that it takes all day. The thing about it taking all day is that it is not a problem since you are on the farm all day anyway. The reason it takes all day is a chicken from the farm starts out the morning alive and ends the evening as bones in a stock pot. The interim is filled by catching, killing, plucking, eviscerating and then cooling your chicken to room temperature. This is followed by collecting the herbs and vegetables from the gardens, and stuffing and trussing the chicken for the oven. I am sure an old hand at this sort of thing could manage much quicker than I ever could. I am also sure that the numbers of folk who are an old hand at this sort of thing are few and far between. Now that we no longer live on the farm it is much easier to roast a chicken but it is not *nearly* as romantic.

    3 ½ - 4 lb whole chicken

    1 sprig rosemary

    2 sprigs thyme

    1 handful Italian parsley

    ¼ boiling onion

    ½ small Danvers carrot

    ½ stick of celery

    ¼ c red wine

    kitchen twine for trussing

    kosher salt

    fresh cracked black pepper

    EVOO

Remove chicken from the refrigerator and bring to room temperature.

Once the chicken has come up to room temperature, pre-heat the oven to 400 degrees. Rinse the chicken in cold water and pat it completely dry with paper towels. Place the herbs and vegetables into the body cavity of the chicken. Use a piece of kitchen twine to truss up the chicken. Place the chicken breast side down in a roasting rack set over a roasting pan. Pour the wine into the body cavity. Salt and pepper the back of the chicken and rub with olive oil. Place in the oven for 25 minutes. Remove the chicken quickly from the oven and turn it over. Salt and pepper the breast side of the chicken and rub with olive oil. Return the chicken to the oven for another 30 minutes. Check for doneness by inserting a thermometer into the thickest part of the thigh next to the breast. It should register 165 degrees when finished. All juices should run clear, NOT pink. Let the chicken rest for 10 minutes before carving to serve. Serve with Israeli couscous with sundried tomatoes and fresh peas (pg. 133) and sautéed French breakfast radishes and steamed spinach (pg. 116).

Bangers and Mash

4 servings

I first ate bangers and mash at a little Irish pub while visiting friends in Olympia, Washington. What a great name for sausages and mashed potatoes served together in a bowl! For such a simple end presentation, I can sure make one heck of a mess in the kitchen preparing this meal. One pot to boil the sausage, a pile of potato peels, one pot to boil and mash the potatoes, one colander to drain the potatoes, a potato masher, a cutting board covered with apple cores and discarded onion parts, a skillet and spatula to fry the onions and apples. All of this scattered in a pile around a simple bowl of sausage and mashed potatoes. But do not let the clean up dissuade you, this is worth every bit.

4 sausages of your choice (bratwurst, Italian, polish, vegetarian)

4 medium russet potatoes

1 large sweet Walla Walla sweet onion

1 tbsp olive oil

1 tsp salt

1 tart Granny Smith apple

2 tsp brown sugar

1 tbsp apple cider vinegar

3 tbsp butter

¼ c whole milk

2 tbsp olive oil

2 tsp salt

fresh ground black pepper

4 tbsp stone ground mustard

Bring a pot of water to boil for the sausages. Bring a second pot of water to boil for the potatoes. Peel and cube the potatoes into large pieces and toss into the second pot. Peel and slice the onion in half and then pole to pole. Add the olive oil to a sauté pan on medium heat and add the onions and the salt. Cook the onions about 10 minutes until they are soft and starting to brown. Add the sausages to the boiling pot on the stove to cook and set a timer to cook until done. Core the Granny Smith apple and cut into bite-sized pieces. Add the apple to the onions in the sauté pan and cook for another 5 minutes. Stir often so the mixture does not burn. Add the brown sugar and cider vinegar to the sauté pan with the onions and apples, and cook for another 5 minutes. While the onions and apples are cooking check on the potatoes by stabbing them with a fork. When they are soft through, drain them in the colander and return them to the cooking pot to mash. Add the butter, milk and olive oil and then mash the potatoes how you like them (smooth or lumpy). Add salt and fresh pepper to taste. Check on the sausages and drain them in the colander when they are cooked through. Return them to the pot to keep warm while you finish up the rest of the cooking (turn the burner off). When the sausages are cooked and drained, the potatoes are mashed and seasoned, the onions and apples are nice and brown and checked for seasoning, you are ready to build your bowl of bangers and mash. In bottom of each bowl place a heaping serving of mashed potatoes. Put one sausage down one side of the bowl, a tablespoon of mustard next to the sausage and a healthy serving of onions and apples over the top of the mashed potatoes. Serve with a green salad and sweet pesto dressing (pg. 53). Enjoy!

Soy Ginger Salmon

2 servings

On my first cooking job in Alaska, I was hired to cook "hearty meals for groups of 20". It was the ease of which I thought I could cook for 20 which drew me to say, yes I want that job, much more than the fact that the job was in Alaska. Now, 20 years later, as I look out my window at the snow covered Chugach Mountains here in Alaska, I am grateful that I was offered the job (and had the good sense to take it!) Once each week, at this job, I would barbecue salmon outdoors on a deck overlooking the Kenai River. The salmon was always marinated overnight in a soy and brown sugar sauce. The guests loved to eat it and the staff always grew weary of salmon by the end of the summer. Now, with a freezer full of salmon, I am happy to eat this variation-on-a-theme marinated salmon every week. At home, I marinate the filets for 30 minutes at a minimum and do not find it necessary to marinate them overnight.

2 - 8oz sockeye salmon filets

¼ c soy sauce

2 cloves Chesnok Red garlic (or substitute other garlic) crushed

2" ginger peeled and roughly chopped

1 tbsp toasted sesame oil

1 tbsp mirin

1 tsp freshly cracked pepper

¼ c water

Mix all the ingredients together in an 8 x 8 pan. Place salmon, skin side up, in the pan with the marinade. Cover and let rest in the fridge for at least 30 minutes. When you are ready to cook the salmon, preheat your oven to 400. Cover a baking sheet with aluminum foil. Remove the salmon from the fridge, and place the filets skin side up on the baking sheet. Place the salmon in the oven and turn the temperature down to 350. Leave in 10 minutes for every inch of thickness. Fish should flake easily with a fork when done. Remove from oven and slide off of the cookie sheet, so as to not continue cooking the fish on the hot pan. Serve with coleslaw (pg. 64) and cornbread with cheddar and jalapenos (pg. 108).

Simple Salmon – Cyprus Smoked Salt & Lemon

4-6 servings

Salmon is a ubiquitous food here in Alaska. This simple preparation is an easy and delicious way to serve salmon to friends and family over and over again. It works equally well in the oven or outside on a grill.

1 whole sockeye salmon filet

juice from one lemon

5-8 lemon slices

2 tsp Cyprus smoked salt (or substitute another smoked salt such as alder or hickory)

Preheat your oven to 400. Rinse the filet and pat dry with paper towels. Place the filet skin side down on a cookie sheet covered with aluminum foil (for easy clean up or easy transfer to the grill outside). Sprinkle the whole fish with lemon juice and Cyprus smoked sea salt. Place lemon slices evenly over the fish. Place the fish in the oven and turn down to 350 degrees. Leave in 10 minutes for every inch of thickness. Fish should flake easily with a fork when done. Remove from oven and slid off the cookie sheet, so as to not continue cooking the fish on the hot pan. Serve with polenta (pg. 103), green beans with salt and oil (pg. 117) and arugula parmesan salad (pg. 63).

Black Bean & Chicken Enchiladas with Roasted Poblano Sauce

6 servings

When given an option for Mexican breakfast, I typically go for the huevos rancheros while my husband prefers chilaquiles. Unlike huevos rancheros, which you can cook up in a flash in the kitchen, these chilaquiles-inspired enchiladas take a bit of time, so plan ahead if you would like to make them. The best chilaquiles sauce I ever tasted was off of Jeff's plate. It was a green creamy poblano sauce served to him somewhere around Puerta Vallarta or maybe it was up in La Paz? I thought it was- hands down- one of the best flavors I have ever tasted. In this recipe, I combine a creamy poblano chilaquiles sauce with corn tortillas, black beans and chicken in a layered lasagna style dish. This dish is easiest to make the same week you roast a chicken so you can use up the leftover chicken. You can also save time by roasting the peppers in the oven with the chicken. I usually roast the peppers and make the poblano sauce one day and then make the enchiladas the next day.

Poblano Sauce

1 large Walla Walla sweet onion

2 tbsp olive oil

4 poblano peppers (roasted, peeled, deveined and seeded)*

2 tbsp flour

1 ¼ c chicken or vegetable broth or water

¼ c sour cream

¼ c cilantro chopped

salt to taste

Chop the onion into bite-sized pieces and sauté in 2 tbsp olive oil until translucent. Chop up the poblano peppers (already roasted, peeled, deveined and seeded) and add them in with the onions. Mix in 2 tablespoon of flour and stir constantly for two minutes. Slowly add the broth of your choice and mix well (no lumps). Cook over medium heat for 5 minutes. Turn off the heat and add the sour cream and cilantro. Use an immersion blender to purée into a smooth sauce. Taste and adjust the seasoning. You can make this a day ahead and store in the refrigerator.

Enchilada Filling

2 c black turtle beans

1 c shredded chicken

1 tsp salt

1 ¾ c Monterey jack cheese

¾ c poblano sauce (see above)

8 corn tortillas

Pre-heat your oven to 350 degrees. In a large bowl, toss the black beans, chicken, salt and 1 ½ cups of Monterey jack cheese with ¾ cup of the poblano sauce. Taste and adjust the seasoning. Cut the corn tortillas in half. In the bottom of a lightly greased 8 x 8 pan, put a layer of the tortillas by matching up the flat edges of the halved tortillas with the flat edges of the pan. Put one half of a tortilla in the middle to cover up the hole. Spread half of the black bean and chicken mixture across the tortillas. Add a second layer of tortillas and the rest of the black bean and chicken mixture. Add a third layer of tortillas. Squash everything good and flat into the pan. Spread the rest of the poblano sauce over the tortillas and sprinkle with cheese. Bake in an oven at 350 degrees for 45 minutes until hot and bubbling. Eat with your favorite salsa or hot sauce. And a side dish of coleslaw with cilantro and lime (pg. 64).

*To Roast the Peppers:

In an oven: Pre-heat your oven to 425 degrees. Wash and dry the peppers. Rub them lightly with oil and set them on a baking sheet. Place the baking sheet on the top rack in your oven. After 18 minutes, rotate the peppers. Roast them for another 12 minutes. When they are finished the skin should be browned and the flesh underneath should be pulling away.

On a grill: Wash and dry the peppers. Set them on a grill over high heat. Keep the peppers turning so as soon as one side is charred you rotate the pepper to keep the flesh underneath from burning. As soon as the peppers are charred all over remove them from the grill.

Peel, seed and de-vein: Put the oven roasted or grilled peppers into a bowl covered with a towel or into a paper bag you roll tightly closed. Allow the peppers to rest for about 10 minutes. One by one, remove the peppers, peel off the skin and discard. Cut open the peppers and remove the veins, seeds and stem. Set aside in a bowl which will collect any juices. Add the peppers and the juices to whatever you are cooking.

Spring Curry from White Star Farms

4 servings

When you have a hoop house, high tunnel or small green house available for use, your fresh produce season really extends from the early spring until late in the fall in cooler climates. Our hoop house plantings started in early February and included carrots, potatoes, arugula, mizuna, lettuce, chard, kale, peas and herbs. Everything was covered in straw and or frost blankets to keep them warm. We could hardly wait to eat these tender young vegetables. As soon as we could gather a handful of snow peas to eat, we would push back the straw and collect a few baby new potatoes, pinch back a few young basil plants and try our luck at finding some baby carrots sturdy enough to add to the meal. A bounty of spring vegetables from out of the hoop houses and into the kitchen! What a magnificent treat.

2 c Basmati rice

2 c. Red Sangre new potatoes (or substitute other new potatoes)

1 c new Danvers carrots (or substitute other carrots)

2 tbsp olive oil

½ c diced yellow onion

2 tbsp diced ginger

2 cloves Polish Softneck garlic (or substitute other garlic)

1 tbsp of your favorite curry powder (or turmeric)

pinch of red chili flakes

1 can coconut milk

¾ c snow peas

½ c young Genovese basil leaves

Cook the basmati rice according to directions. Cut the new potatoes and carrots into bite size pieces. Steam the vegetables gently with ¾ cup of water in a covered sauté pan until almost tender. Remove the lid and allow the water to evaporate. In the meantime, finely dice the yellow onion, ginger and garlic. Add the olive oil, onion, ginger, and garlic. Sauté until the onion is tender. Add the curry powder and red chili flakes and sauté until fragrant. Add one can of coconut milk and 1/2c. water. Bring to a simmer and salt to taste. Turn off the heat. Slice the snow peas into bite-sized pieces and add to the curry. Tear the basil leaves into bite-sized pieces and add them to the curry. Stir gently until warmed through. Serve over basmati rice. Kick up the heat with Siracha. Enjoy this perfect one bowl meal!

Fish Cakes with Brown Rice and Lemon Sauce

4 servings

Back when I was teaching, a co-worker gave me a recipe for crab cakes one day. She had made them the night before and thought they were just perfect. I no longer have that recipe and I never did make those crab cakes but, if I recall correctly, they had a combined quantity in cups plural of heavy cream and mayonnaise. No wonder they were good. Later when living in Japan and always having a) fish on hand and b) panko bread crumbs, I used to make these fish cakes for dinner on a regular basis. They are perfectly delicious.

2 c brown rice

1 lb white fish (halibut, rock fish, cod or any leftover fish from dinner last night)

¾ c soy sauce

1 tsp black pepper

1 tsp granulated garlic

water

½ c plain yogurt

1 tbsp lemon juice

1 tsp sugar

pinch of table salt

1 ½ c panko

¼ c mayonnaise

1 drop liquid smoke

2 tbsp chives

¼ tsp salt

¼ tsp pepper

½ tsp granulated garlic

2 tbsp olive oil

Cook the brown rice according to directions.

If you have any leftover cooked fish, you can use that. If not, you can prepare it this way: Mix the soy sauce, black pepper and granulated garlic together in a small shallow pan. Add the fish skin side up and add enough water to just cover the fish. Leave to marinate for 30 minutes. Turn on the broiler in your oven. Remove the fish from the marinade and place on a baking sheet. Place the fish under the broiler and broil until cooked through. This should only take a few minutes. Please keep one eye on the fish until you turn the broiler off and remove it from the oven.

In a bowl mix the yogurt, lemon juice, sugar and pinch of salt. Set aside.

Shred the cooked fish into a bowl and add the panko, mayonnaise, liquid smoke, chopped chives, salt, pepper and garlic. Form the fish mixture into balls about the size of a golf ball and then squash into a patty. Fry the cakes in a pan coated with olive oil until brown on both sides and warmed through. Server over a bed of brown rice drizzled with lemon sauce and a side of hearty spring greens (pg. 114).

Spring Rolls with Tofu and Peanut Sauce

3 servings

Some years ago, after multiple weeks traveling with a friend, we decided to stay put for awhile, in the historical town of Luang Pruabang in Laos. Here we found perfect weather, a slow pace, more than enough temples to visit and some of the nicest cafes and street food of the trip. We returned over and over again to one little place for lunch and take out… just to eat their spring rolls one more time. In fact, the morning we left on the bus headed back to the capitol, we picked up our last order to take with us for bus lunch. Here is how I make spring rolls at home. They are almost as good as I remember.

1 container firm tofu drained and slice into thin sticks ~ 3" x ¾ " x ½ "

2 tbsp olive oil

2 tbsp soy sauce

1 tbsp nutritional yeast powder

1 clump mung bean noodles (~ 1 c cooked)

6 leaves Black Seeded Simpson green lettuce (or substitute other tender green leaf lettuce)

3 Evergreen Hardy White scallions cut into 3" lengths

1 small seeded cucumber cut into 3" lengths and sliced about the diameter of your small finger

6 sprigs cilantro

6 spring roll wrappers

Peanut Sauce

¼ c creamy peanut butter

2 tbsp water

2 tbsp soy sauce

1 tbsp seasoned rice wine vinegar

1 tsp siracha

dash of Vietnamese cinnamon

In a large skillet, fry the tofu in oil over medium heat until brown on both sides. Add the soy sauce and nutritional yeast and toss to coat. Continue to fry until the soy sauce has evaporated. Remove from heat and set aside. Cook the mung beans noodles by tossing them into a pot of boiling water, turning off the heat and letting them rest for 3 minutes. Then drain the noodles and cool them under cold running water. Set the noodles aside. Prepare the vegetables by washing and cutting into 3" lengths. Set these aside.

Fill a pie pan with about 1" of water. One at a time swirl a spring roll wrapper around in the water until it starts to become flexible. Remove it from the water, shake off the excess and set it on a cutting board. As the water absorbs into the wrapper it should become more and more flexible. In the center of the wrapper, place a lettuce leaf (folded so the edges of the wrapper have no filling), pieces of tofu, green onion, a sprig of cilantro, and cucumber slices. Gently, but tightly wrap it all up like a burrito, folding in the outer edges and rolling as you go. Continue until all six rolls have been made.

While the rolls are resting, whip up the peanut dipping sauce. In a small mixing bowl add the peanut butter, soy sauce, rice wine vinegar, water, siracha and dash of cinnamon. Whisk these ingredients together until you have a smooth sauce. Taste and adjust the seasoning as you see fit.

Serve.

Summer Squash Fritters (Super Easy or Fancy)

4 servings

While working on our friend's farm one summer, we happened to be there during the peak of summer squash season. One of our jobs was to harvest the squash daily, to store for the weekly markets. Jeff and I would take turns walking the long rows and filling totes with patty pans, crooknecks, zucchini, eight balls and the like. No matter how carefully we checked each row of plants for ripe fruits we would on occasion miss just one. The next day you would be treated to a county fair, blue ribbon specimen, now protruding from the home plate sized leaf under which it was hiding yesterday. The only thing to do was take them home, shred them up and eat as many fritters as possible. I look forward to squash fritter season every summer.

Super Easy Fritters

Mix up a batch of pancake mix according to package directions. Shred an equal amount of squash into the mix (2 c mixed up mix + 2 c squash). Add a pinch of salt and some fresh cracked pepper. Fry up on a griddle and serve with ketchup and sour cream.

Fancy Fritters

2 c shredded summer squash (any combination of cocozelle, Benning's Green Tint patty pan, crookneck, etc.)

¼ c diced Rossa di Milano red onion (or substitute other red onion)

2 eggs

1 bunch chives

¼ c shredded parmesan reggiano

½ tsp salt

¼ c water

Topping

2 beefsteak tomatoes (such as Kellogg's Breakfast or Moskvich)

2 tbsp EVOO

alder smoked salt(or substitute other smoked salt)

sour cream

Add all of the ingredients for the fritters to a bowl. Mix well and let rest for 3 minutes. Mix again and cook on a griddle set to medium. Dice and seed the fresh tomatoes and place into a small bowl. Drizzle with the olive oil, stir and set aside. Serve the squash fritters on a plate with a generous scoop of diced tomatoes, a sprinkling of Cyprus smoked salt and a dollop of sour cream.

Poached Rockfish with Vegetable Relish

2 servings

Rockfish of one type or another was the most frequently caught fish off the small tourism boat I worked on in Southeast Alaska. The captain would usually beer batter and fry the fish for appetizers, which was delicious. Once, on the farm, someone gave us a little bit of rockfish. I made this dish as a light and quick way to enjoy rockfish and fresh veggies from the garden or farmers market.

¼ c Italian parsley

½ c beefsteak tomato diced (such as Brandywine, Cherokee Purple, Moskvich)

¼ c Rosa di Milano purple onion diced

1 tbsp EVOO

kosher salt

1 c water

½ lemon juiced

¼ c vermouth

3 sprigs Italian parsley

1 small shallot

1 bay leaf

1 ½ tsp kosher salt

2 black peppercorns

½ lb rockfish fillet

Entrées

In a small bowl, mix together chopped parsley, seeded and diced tomato, finely diced purple onion, EVOO and a pinch of kosher salt. Taste and adjust seasoning then set aside. In a large sauté pan with a well-fitting lid, place the water, lemon juice, vermouth, parsley, diced shallot, bay, kosher salt and peppercorns. Bring to a boil and let simmer for 5 minutes. Bring back to a boil and add the rockfish. Turn the heat down to medium and cover with a lid. Check the fish after 5 minutes for doneness. Cover and cook a few minutes longer if necessary. Be careful not to overcook. Serve immediately with a pile of relish on top and fresh cracked pepper. Serve with spinach salad (pg. 73) and sweet potato mash with coconut and lime (pg. 111).

Skillet Cooked Peppered Tri-tip with Gremolata

2 servings

A very nice beer brewery out of San Diego spent eleven years producing a series of special beers. One was released each year in consecutive months starting on February 2, 2002 and culminating on December 12, 2012. Jeff and I bought and cellared these beers and in March of 2014 we finally pulled off our tasting party. By the time the party rolled around we realized we only had a flight of 2004 to 2012 to serve. The year 2002 was one bottle we never did get our hands on and the only bottle of 2003 we had was consumed by us sometime in 2013! The tasting part of this party paired each bottle with a bite-sized snack. The year 2005 had flavors of chocolate, dried fruit, anise and coffee to name a few. We paired this with the below skillet cooked peppered tri-tip with gremolata. I had originally intended to just serve the peppered tri-tip but at the last minute tossed together the gremolata and found it to be a perfect match. This peppered tri-tip is quick to cook. You can get everything else ready for dinner and then toss this into the skillet at the last minute.

1 lb tri-tip cut into 2 x 11/2 " strips

2 tsp finely ground black pepper (almost a powder)

2 tsp kosher salt

olive oil

Gremolata:

1/3 c finely chopped Italian parsley leaves

2 cloves Chesnok Red garlic

½-1 tsp lemon zest

1 ½ tbsp EVOO

Maldon salt (for finishing)

Bring the tri-tip up to room temperature. In the meantime, finely chop the parsley and add it to a small mixing bowl. Crush the garlic cloves through a press and add them to the parsley along with the lemon zest and EVOO. Mix these ingredients together well and set aside. Rub a generous amount of pepper and salt into the tri-tip strips. Heat 1 tablespoon of olive oil in a cast iron skillet on medium high until it shimmers. Add the tri-tip. Allow to cook for about 3 minutes per side, or adjust for desired doneness. Pull off of the heat and let rest on the cutting board for a few minutes. Slice into bite-sized wafers. Pile onto a serving platter cover with the gremolata and sprinkle with a bit of Maldon salt.

DESSERTS

Barbecue Apple

Blackberry Cream Galette with Marzipan

Raspberry, Goat Cheese and Rosemary Galette

Dark Chocolate Salt Carmel Cookies

Rhubarb Buckle

"Black Bottom" Carrot Cupcakes

Chocolate Chip Cookies with Coconut

Magic Mexican Molten Cake

Barbecue Apple

8 x 8 pan

I used to make this when we were running the barbecue all afternoon on the farm in the fall. Plunk a couple of apples from the orchard on the grill, and dessert would roast away while we worked. Roasting apples is also very easy to do in your oven at home, especially when you are already cooking something in the oven for dinner. This dessert is simple and so very good to eat.

> 2 apples (a sturdy variety which will not go all to mush when cooking: Granny Smith, Honeycrisp, Fuji, Braeburn)
>
> ¼ c honey
>
> ¼ c cream
>
> 2 tbsp Vietnamese cinnamon
>
> ¼ c toasted walnuts

Pre-heat your oven to 350 degrees. Cut the apples in half and remove the core. Place in an 8 x8 baking dish, cut side down. Add water to the dish until it comes just up to the core of the apples. Cover tightly with foil and place in the oven for about 35 minutes until the apples are very nice and soft.

When the apples have finished baking it is time to toast the walnuts in a skillet on top of the stove. When the walnuts have browned nicely, turn off the heat and add the honey and cinnamon. When the honey has melted and you have stirred and mixed the ingredients together in the pan, add the cream. Stir again until uniform. Remove the apples from the baking dish and place each half cut side up into a small dessert bowl. Pour the cream and honey sauce over each apple. Sprinkle with cinnamon and serve warm.

(Add a 1 tsp of bourbon along with the honey for a chilly autumn evening kick.)

Blackberry Cream Galette with Marzipan

1 - 8" galette

When I first started working after college, I lived in a house on the side of a small mountain in a neighborhood at the edge of town. Three quarters of the mountain was covered with woods, and an empty field on the backside had a lovely pond to walk around. There was an old abandoned and overgrown homestead on the front side, mostly notable for the apple orchard which still produced all the apples I ever wanted for putting up apple sauce in the fall. Between our house and the apple orchard, there was an old road which was almost overgrown with Himalayan blackberries. While a little on the seedy side, they were abundant and easy to pick. So, many early fall afternoons I would set out for my walk with a small bucket to collect some blackberries to freeze for the winter. Over the years, I have experimented with blackberry pies, jams, stratas, smoothies, crisps and cobblers. I made this treat one day for Jeff. It is just the ticket for blackberries. I hope you like it as well.

Galette Dough

makes enough for 2 - 8" galettes

1 ¼ c flour

½ tsp salt

6 tbsp butter

2 tbsp cream cheese

6-8 tbsp ice water

½ tsp lemon juice

Add the flour and salt to a medium size mixing bowl and stir to make a uniform mixture. Cut the butter and cream cheese into teaspoon sized pieces and toss with the flour to coat. Using your fingertips and working quickly, flatten and break apart the pieces of butter and cream cheese. In a small bowl, measure ½ c of water and add an ice cube or two and ½ tsp lemon juice. Start by adding 4 tablespoons of water to the flour and fat mixture. Toss it around with a fork and then add 2 more tablespoons of water and toss. Continue until the dough is damp and you can pinch it together. You do not need to add water until a ball has formed. Pour the dough out onto a counter and knead it gently several times until it all comes together in one nice lump. Separate the dough into two balls and wrap them in plastic wrap. Flatten each ball into a disk and chill for at least one hour before rolling out.

Remove the dough from the fridge, unwrap it and place it between two sheets of parchment paper. Using a rolling pin, roll the dough into a 9" circle. Peel away the top sheet of parchment paper and using a pizza wheel trim the edges so they are nice and pretty. Set the parchment paper with the dough onto a cookie sheet.

Topping

1 ½ cup fresh or frozen blackberries

1 tbsp sugar

¼ c almond flour

¼ tsp almond extract

2 tbsp sour cream

2 tbsp sugar

pinch of table salt

2 tsp turbinado sugar

Preheat your oven to 400 degrees. Toss the blackberries with the sugar in a small bowl and set aside. In a second small bowl add the almond flour, almond extract, sour cream, sugar and pinch of salt. Mix these together well and then spread across the rolled out galette dough leaving 1" around the outer edge free of this topping. Dump the blackberries and sugar in the middle of the galette and then spread out in one even layer over the sour cream and almond flour mixture. Fold the edges of the dough up over the filling pinching them together as they overlap. When you are finished you should have an 8"circle with 1" of pinched up dough on the outside and 7" of glistening, sugar coated blackberries on the inside. Using a pastry brush, brush the 1" rim of dough with cold water and then sprinkle it with turbinado sugar. Bake in on the center rack in your oven for 35 minutes. The galette is done when the bottom and edges have browned nicely.

Raspberry, Goat Cheese and Rosemary Galette

1 - 8" galette

If I make the previous blackberry almond galette for Jeff, I make this raspberry rosemary galette for me. The raspberry is my favorite berry. It has been for as long as I can remember. I can walk by strawberries all year and never care if I get one. But raspberries have got me hook, line and sinker. Growing up, we had a very nice berry patch and I remember standing in among the raspberry canes eating the berries in the summer. When I cooked at summer camp, down by the lake there was a patch of raspberries with berries as big as the end of my thumb. I would hustle the other cook and the dishwashers out the back door of the kitchen, bowls in hand, just after dinner was served to go pick a pile of raspberries for *our* dinner. We would sneak back in and put heaping spoonfuls of sweet whipping cream over the berries in our bowls and sigh at just how good life could be sometimes.

Galette Dough (see recipe page 174)

Topping

1 ½ c fresh or frozen raspberries

1 tbsp sugar

2 oz goat cheese

1 tbsp chopped fresh rosemary

1 tsp black salt (or kosher salt)

Prepare one 8" round of galette dough as described on page 176.

Preheat your oven to 400 degrees. In a small bowl, toss the raspberries and sugar and set aside. In a second small bowl mix together the goat cheese and the rosemary. Spread the cheese mixture onto the galette dough, leaving a 1" ring of dough around the outer edge. Dump the raspberries onto the cheese mixture and spread them out into a single uniform layer. Fold up the outer edge of the galette over the berries, pinching it as you go. Brush water on the outer edge of dough using a pastry brush. Sprinkle the dough with black salt. Bake in on the center rack in your oven for 35 minutes. The galette is done when the bottom and edges have browned nicely.

Dark Chocolate Salt Caramel Cookies

2 dozen cookies

I love caramels. Not caramel sauce, but creamy and chewy caramels. For the most part, caramels show up on Halloween. Little cubes wrapped in cellophane or flat disks you can wrap around apples on a stick. In general, the caramel on apples fits the creamy chewy caramel parameters, but for whatever reason the apples used underneath, in my experience, have never, ever been very tasty. Which is too bad, because what a nice combination apples and caramels make, don't you think? In the past few years I have noticed cellophane wrapped caramels here and there showing up as hand made by small boutique candy shops. Yum. And salted caramels seem to appear with as much regularity as salted chocolates. And so here is a cookie which takes the caramel, chocolate and salt, forgets all about the apples, and makes a very satisfying caramel treat for any time of year.

½ c + 2 tbsp butter melted and cooled

1 ½ c flour

½ tsp baking powder

¼ tsp baking soda

¼ tsp table salt

½ c + 2 tbsp cocoa powder

1 c white sugar

2 tsp vanilla

2 eggs

12 soft caramels

1 tbsp kosher salt

Preheat the oven to 350 degrees. In a small skillet or microwave, melt the butter and set aside in a large mixing bowl to cool. In a small mixing bowl, add the flour, baking powder, baking soda, salt and cocoa powder. Sift these dry ingredients together. Once the butter has cooled, add the sugar and whisk until light in color. Add the vanilla and then the eggs one at a time and incorporate with the sugar and butter. Pour the dry flour mixture into the wet butter mixture and stir with a spoon until well blended. Scoop the dough into walnut sized pieces and place on an ungreased cookie sheet. Unwrap and cut each caramel in half. Press one half of a caramel into the top of each cookie. Bake for 10-12 minutes. Allow to cool on the baking sheet for about 2 minutes then transfer to a rack to cool completely. Caution: right out of the oven, the caramel will be much to hot to eat!
.

Rhubarb Buckle

8 x 8 pan

One of the foods my mother made from the garden when I was a child was rhubarb sauce. I have always remembered the taste of this sauce and was delighted one day to discover, when talking to my oldest brother that he also remembered and loved to eat rhubarb sauce. It is always nice to share a memory with a sibling, and better yet to both have the same feeling about the same memory. To this day, I love the tart flavor of rhubarb. The addition of warming cinnamon to this rhubarb buckle is just out of this world.

- 3 c rhubarb (in ½" slices) (if using frozen rhubarb, thaw first)
- 2 tbsp corn starch
- 3 tbsp brown sugar
- ¼ tsp table salt
- 2 tbsp butter (melted)
- ¾ c flour
- ½ c sugar
- 2 tsp Vietnamese cinnamon
- 2 tsp baking powder
- ½ c milk

Preheat the oven to 350 degrees. Toss the rhubarb, cornstarch, brown sugar and salt together in a bowl. Set the rhubarb mixture aside. In another bowl, mix together the melted butter, flour, sugar, cinnamon, baking powder and milk. Pour batter into a greased 8 x 8" baking pan. Scoop fruit mixture over the top of the batter and gently press into one even layer. Bake in the oven for 45 minutes. The buckle is done when a toothpick inserted in the center comes out clean.

"Black Bottom" Carrot Cupcakes

15 cupcakes

Those gooey chocolaty cupcakes with cream cheese and chocolate chips on the bottom were, for years, my favorite cupcake. With the rise of the cupcake over the last few years, I thought to myself one day, "What kind of cupcake would I make for a cupcake shop?" This thought sprang almost immediately into my head and I wrote it down. It was not until putting this cookbook together that I actually worked out a recipe and made a batch. They turned out to be perfectly delicious and I had to share.

<u>Filling</u>

8 oz cream cheese

1 egg

1/3 c sugar

pinch of table salt

2 tbsp finely diced crystallized ginger

In a small mixing bowl blend the cream cheese, egg, sugar and salt until smooth. Fold in the finely diced crystallized ginger. Set aside.

<u>Cupcakes</u>

1 ½ c flour

1 c sugar

1 tsp soda

½ tsp salt

1 tsp Vietnamese cinnamon

1 c water

1/3 c oil

3 tbsp white vinegar

1 tsp vanilla

1 c Danvers carrot grated

Preheat your oven to 350 degrees. Mix the dry ingredients together in a medium mixing bowl. Mix the water, oil, egg, vinegar and vanilla together in a small mixing bowl. Add the wet to the dry and mix them together. Gently fold in the shredded carrots.

Line a muffin tin with paper liners. Fill each paper liner 2/3 c full of batter. Add 2 tbsp of the cream cheese mixture to the top of each muffin. Bake on the center rack of your oven for about 18 minutes.

Chocolate Chip Cookies with Coconut

2 ½ dozen cookies

My dad tells the story of how his older sister would make chocolate chip cookies for the family when he was a kid. In order to keep them from being eaten up quickly, his mom would have the cookies placed in a cookie jar and his older brother, who was 6'5", would put the cookie jar above the cupboards in the kitchen. Now, since Dad had four grown older brothers who were over 6 feet tall, I wonder if Dad was the only one who could not get into those cookies! I myself, after years of baking chocolate chip cookies, have come to think they taste better with coconut. You might too.

2 ¼ c flour

½ tsp baking powder

½ tsp baking soda

½ tsp salt

1 c butter

¾ c brown sugar

½ c white sugar

2 eggs

2 tsp vanilla

1 c chocolate chips

½ c shredded coconut

Preheat your oven to 325 degrees. In a small mixing bowl add the flour, baking powder, baking soda and salt together. Mix well and set aside. In a metal bottomed skillet (not non-stick), brown ¾ c of butter. Do not leave this unattended, lest it burn. Pour this browned butter and all the browned bits into a large mixing bowl, add ¼ c cold butter and cut into tablespoon sized pieces. Stir until this cold butter has melted and the whole bowl has cooled. Add the sugar and whisk to fully incorporate and lighten in color. When the sugar butter mixture is cool enough that it will not cook the eggs, add them one at a time and whisk to incorporate. Add the vanilla and mix. Pour this mixture over the dry flour mixture and stir to fully incorporate. Fold in the chocolate chips and coconut. Place 2 tbsp sized balls of dough on an ungreased cookie sheet and bake for 12-15 minutes. Cool on a wire rack.

Magic Mexican Molten Cake

8 x 8 pan

I remember my mom making a magic cake in the kitchen when I was growing up. It was magic because she would dump all this stuff into the baking pan and stir and then toss it in the oven to bake. What came out of the oven was an amazing chocolate cake with hot fudge sauce underneath! How on earth did something so amazing happen in the oven? Cake and hot fudge sauce all in one pan together? This was really a piece of kitchen magic. As an adult, I have made this cake at the last minute when feeding a hungry construction crew. There are no eggs in this cake so it is a good back pocket recipe to have on hand (for when you want a dessert but are out of eggs). Naturally, chocolate cake and hot fudge sauce do go perfectly with vanilla ice cream. And to keep things interesting to your palate, I have added cinnamon and spicy chili powder. Let the magic begin again.

1 c flour

½ c white sugar

3 tbsp cocoa powder

2 tsp baking powder

¼ tsp salt

2 tsp cinnamon

¼ tsp hot chili pepper powder (plus or minus your choice)

½ c milk

2 tbsp olive oil

2 tbsp vanilla

¾ c brown sugar

¼ c cocoa powder

1 ¾ c boiling water

Preheat your oven to 350 degrees. In an 8 x 8 baking pan, use a fork to mix together the flour, sugar, cocoa powder, baking powder, salt, cinnamon and chili powder. In a small mixing bowl whisk together the milk, olive oil, and vanilla. Pour this into the baking pan and mix until uniform with a fork. Spread this thick dough out over the whole pan. Sprinkle the brown sugar and cocoa powder evenly over the mixture in the pan. Pour 1 ¾ c just boiled water over the whole thing and put it in the oven to bake for 40 minutes. Let it cool enough when you take it out of the oven so that you do not burn your tongue on the hot fudge sauce! Serve with vanilla ice cream, whipped cream or even just a blop of whipping cream straight from the carton.

Recipe & DF, GF, V Index

DF = Dairy Free*, **GF** = Gluten Free**, **V** = Vegetarian (no meat)

*some recipes can be made dairy free with the removal of a dairy topping (cheese, sour cream etc.), or use of olive oil instead of butter

**some recipes need substitutions of a gluten free cracker or use of tamari in place of soy sauce

Appetizers, 7

Sumo Snacks **(V)**, 9

Pico de Gallo and Salsa **(DF, GF, V)**, 10

Mizuna Pesto with Ricotta **(V)**, 12

Pita Wedges Two Ways **(V)**, 14

Roasted Red Pepper Spread **(GF, V)**, 16

Rosemary Crackers with Goat Cheese and Fresh Plums **(V)**, 17

Grilled Eggplant Dip **(DF, GF, V)**, 18

Spring Radish Spread **(GF, V)**, 20

Mushroom Gyoza **(DF, V)**, 21

Pesto Cheese Bundles **(V)**, 23

Popcorn **(DF, GF, V)**, 25

Breakfast, 27

Breakfast Strata Sweet or Savory **(V)**, 29

Biscuits with Peppered Mushroom Gravy **(V)**, 32

Scones Sweet or Savory **(V)**, 34

Sweet Pumpkin Bread with Ginger **(DF, V)**, 36

Summer Squash Bread **(DF, V)**, 38

Hashbrowns **(DF, GF, V)**, 40

Fabulous Muffins (Cherry, Coconut, Carrot, Cinnamon) **(V)**, 41

Farmer's Skillet New Potatoes **(DF, GF, V)**, 43

Huevos Rancheros **(DF, GF, V)**, 45

French Toast **(V)**, 47

Banana Walnut Pancakes **(V)**, 48

Salad Dressings, 51

Sweet Pesto Dressing **(GF, V)**, 53

Farm Ranch Dressing **(GF, V)**, 54

Chipotle Mayo **(DF, GF, V)**, 55

Thousand Island or Fry Sauce **(DF, GF, V)**, 56

Japanese Citrus Dressing **(DF, V)**, 57

Miso Dressing **(DF, GF, V)**, 58

Classic Vinaigrette **(DF, GF, V)**, 59

Salads, 61

Arugula Parmesan **(GF, V)**, 63

Coleslaw with Variations **(DF, GF, V)**, 64

Tuscan Kale Salad **(V)**, 66

Little Gems with Strawberries **(DF, GF, V)**, 67

Mizuna and Tofu Salad **(DF, V)**, 68

Speckled Amish Bib with Goat Cheese & Raspberries **(GF, V)**, 69

Iceberg Wedge Salad **(GF, V)**, 70

Panzanella **(V)**, 71

Spinach Salad **(DF, GF, V)**, 73

Corn Salad **(DF, GF, V)**, 74

Greek Salad **(DF, GF, V)**, 76

Soups and Sandwiches, 79

Lentil Stew with Parsley Dumplings **(V)**, 81

White Star Farms Gazpacho **(GF, V)**, 83

Cream of Celery with Havarti **(V)**, 85

Two Bean Chili **(DF, GF, V)**, 87

Red Rhubarb Chard Quesadillas **(GF, V)**, 89

Arugula Chicken Salad on Ciabatta, **91**

Bratwurst with Roasted Onion and Sauerkraut Relish on Hoagie Rolls **(DF, V)**, 92

Three Cheese with Chips on Whole Wheat Toast **(V)**, 94

Wilted Spinach Croissant **(V)**, 96

Tofu Sliders with Wasabi Mayonnaise **(DF, V)**, 98

Sides, 101

Polenta with Variations **(DF, GF, V)**, 103

Home Fries **(DF, GF, V)**, 105

Risotto with Mushrooms and Vermouth **(GF, V)**, 106

Cornbread with Cheddar and Jalapenos **(V)**, 108

French Lentil with Spring Herbs **(DF, GF, V)**, 110

Sweet Potato Mash with Coconut and Lime **(DF, GF, V)**, 111

Cabbage Pancakes **(DF, V)**, 112

Hearty Spring Greens Seven Ways **(DF, GF, V)**, 114

Sautéed French Breakfast Radishes with Steamed Spinach **(GF, V)**, 116

Green Beans with Salt and Oil **(DF, GF, V)**, 117

Pasta & Pizza, 119

Orecchiette with Parsley and Garlic **(DF, V)**, 121

Angel Hair with Swiss Chard and Peanuts **(DF, V)**, 123

Tuscan Kale Carbonara, **125**

Fava Beans and Chive Blossom Bulgur **(DF, GF, V)**, 127

Simmered Red Sauce from Canned Tomato **(DF, GF, V)**, 129

Blue Cheese & Walnut Garden Fresh Linguini **(V)**, 131

Israeli Couscous with Sun-dried Tomatoes and Fresh Peas **(DF, V)**, 133

Spicy Cold Soba Salad **(DF, V)**, 134

Mushroom Pizza **(V)**, 136

Caramelized Onion and Smoked Blue Cheese Pizza **(V)**, 139

Spinach & Three Cheese Calzone **(V)**, 141

Entrées, 145

Roast Chicken **(DF, GF)**, 147

Bangers and Mash **(V)**, 149

Soy Ginger Salmon **(DF, GF)**, 151

Simple Salmon – Cyprus Smoked Salt & Lemon**(DF, GF)**, 153

Black Bean & Chicken Enchiladas with Roasted Poblano Sauce, 154

Spring Curry from White Star Farms **(DF, GF, V)**, 157

Fish Cakes with Brown Rice and Lemon Sauce, 159

Spring Rolls with Tofu and Peanut Sauce **(DF, GF, V)**, 161

Summer Squash Fritters (Super Easy or Fancy) **(V)**, 163

Poached Rockfish with Vegetable Relish **(DF, GF)**, 165

Skillet Cooked Peppered Tri-tip with Gremolata **(DF, GF)**, 167

Desserts, 171

Barbecue Apple **(GF, V)**, 173

Blackberry Cream Galette with Marzipan **(V)**, 174

Raspberry, Goat Cheese and Rosemary Galette **(V)**, 177

Dark Chocolate Salt Carmel Cookies **(V)**, 179

Rhubarb Buckle **(V)**, 181

"Black Bottom" Carrot Cupcakes **(V), 183**

Chocolate Chip Cookies with Coconut **(V), 185**

Magic Mexican Molten Cake **(V), 187**

Heirloom Index

Basil	Genovese, 14, 157
Bean (dried)	Black Turtle, 45, 89, 155
Bean (pole)	Kentucky Wonder, 117
Cabbage (green)	Early Jersey Wakefield, 64, 65
Cabbage (savoy)	Des Vertus, 112
Carrot	Danvers, 21, 41, 81, 112, 147, 184
Chive	Nira, 21
Cinnamon	Vietnamese, 36, 38, 41, 162, 173, 181, 184
Eggplant	Rosa Bianca, 18
Garlic	Polish Softneck, 121, 127, 157
Garlic	Chesnok Red 129, 151, 167
Green (Asian)	Mizuna, 12, 68
Green (peppery)	Arugula, 63, 64, 91
Kale	Tuscan, 66, 125
Lettuce	Little Gems, 67
Lettuce	Speckled Amish Bib, 69
Lettuce	Black Seeded Simpson, 71, 94, 98, 161
Onion (red)	Rosa di Milano, 70, 73, 76, 105, 165
Onion (sweet)	Walla Walla, 43, 71, 92, 106, 140, 149, 154
Potato	Bintje, 43

Potato	Red Sangre, 157
Prunes	Purple Italian, 17
Pumpkin	Marina di Chioggia, 36
Radish	French Breakfast, 20, 68, 116
Scallion	Evergreen Hardy White, 20, 21, 74, 83, 89, 108, 112, 124, 134, 161
Summer Squash	Benning's Green Tint (patty pan), 38, 163
Summer Squash	Crookneck, 38, 163
Swiss Chard	Red Rhubarb, 89, 123, 134
Tomato (mini)	Red Pear, 71, 74, 131
Tomato (mini)	Principe Borghese, 133
Tomato (slicing)	Brandywine, 10, 76, 83, 91, 94, 165
Tomato (slicing)	Cherokee Purple, 10, 76, 83, 91, 94, 165
Tomato (slicing)	Moskvich, 10, 76, 83, 98, 165
Tomato (slicing)	Kellogg's Breakfast, 94, 98
Zucchini	Cocozelle, 38, 163
Zucchini	Costata Romanesca, 14

www.ingramcontent.com/pod-product-compliance
Lightning Source LLC
Chambersburg PA
CBHW080541170426
43195CB00016B/2634